The Peace That Passes All Misunderstanding

By Thomas E. Witherspoon

Unity Books
Unity Village, MO 64065

Part I

Part II

Promises to Keep

Part III

Dedication

In the fourth chapter of Philippians, Paul told us of: ". . . *the peace of God, which passes all understanding.*"

Someone (no one knows for sure just who) changed this phrase to: The peace of God, which passes all *misunderstanding*. Both sayings ring true, for real and lasting peace does pass all understanding and misunderstanding.

This book is about peace. It is about peace of mind, primarily, but it also deals with peace in relationships, peace among nations, and universal peace.

It is appropriate that Unity publish such a book when many people find peace of mind an elusive quality. Many are convinced that the only peace they will attain is in death. This is untrue. Peace is possible in all hearts and minds. We live in a good world full of good people and our God is absolute good. Peace prevails in the lives of many people; it can prevail in the lives of all.

This book is dedicated to the men and women who have written for Unity School of Christianity for some 100 years. Every writer, and there have been thousands, has contributed to peace in all its aspects.

"Glory to God in the highest, and on earth peace among men with whom he is well pleased" (Lk. 2:14).

Notes On Peace

"Peace cannot be kept by force. It can only be achieved by understanding."—Albert Einstein

"Only the just man enjoys peace of mind."—Epicurus

"War is an invention of the human mind. The human mind can invent peace with justice."—Norman Cousins

"Our goal must be—not peace in our time—but peace for all time."—Harry Truman

"Man's whole character is determined by the thoughts for which he allows a place in his mind. A strong man or a weak man is what he is because of repeated thoughts of strength or weakness. Steadfast affirmations of peace will harmonize the whole body structure and open the way to attainment of healthy conditions in mind and body."—Charles Fillmore

"Peace I leave with you; my peace I give to you; not as the world gives do I give to you. Let not your hearts be troubled, neither let them be afraid" (Jn. 14:27).—Jesus Christ

Part One

The Peace That Passes All Misunderstanding

A young man, approaching the end of his college experience and preparing to enter the world of business, made a list of all the things he hoped to achieve in his career. The list included fame, fortune, good relationships, power, health, success and rapid advancement in management, and an array of other good things. When the list was completed, he took it to a professor and asked for his opinion of the goals. The professor, a very old soul in terms of wisdom, shocked the young man by drawing a huge X through the list.

"You are a victim of misunderstanding," the professor declared. Then he wrote on the paper, in large black letters, PEACE OF MIND.

"Peace of mind is the most important goal of all. It should top your list, for without it, these other things will become a hideous torment to you," the professor added.

The young man immediately knew the truth of what he had been told. He left with determination and a new objective in life, and ultimately achieved all these things. His misunderstanding turned into perfect understanding, and his success was thus assured.

Isn't this what Jesus Christ taught us?

"But seek first his kingdom and his righteousness, and all these things shall be yours as well" (Mt. 6:33).

Fame, fortune, success, good health, power, and all other such attributes are "things." The kingdom is where peace dwells. And where peace dwells, all things can be achieved.

Unity believes the kingdom is that realm in consciousness in which we know and understand God. It is the Christ within each of us, operating as our higher self and directing divine ideas to us.

Jesus Christ told us that the kingdom is at

hand, or in our very midst, and that in effect we have but to take hold of it and it is ours, right now. If we do, perfect peace and harmony are ours.

Surely each of us must come to an understanding that heaven cannot be postponed until this life ends. Heaven is available right now. This very knowledge is the key to our peace of mind. The diligent pursuit of heaven right now assures it.

Peace of mind is available to each human being in direct proportion to each human being's desire for it and initiative in achieving it. Desire is but the first part of this worthy goal. Initiative is the larger part. A sacrifice is absolutely essential in every peace of mind situation. What is the sacrifice? Negative thinking and feeling must be eliminated. There is no other route to peace of mind. There is no other method to achieve world peace. All misunderstanding must be transformed into understanding. The torment of misunderstanding must be transformed into the peace of understanding.

Peace of mind is a possession that belongs only to precious few human beings who have come to this conclusion and have taken positive, creative action to achieve that which has for so long eluded them. Peace of mind need not be so elusive. It is a gift from God, equally available to all God's children. God does not favor one child over another, nor give good to one and not to another. God is not a dispenser of good; God is the source of good. Each one of us draws from God's vast reservoir the exact amount of good that we lay claim to. God's good is akin to a giant smorgasbord of good things to eat and drink. Everyone is invited to the banquet. Each one may take what he or she wants. The positive, loving, and creative child of God knows he deserves the best. He moves forward and claims his good. The negative and unimaginative child of God stays back, reluctant to claim his good. He feels unworthy, undeserving, and thus misses out on the good that God wants everyone to have.

Whose fault is this? Why should anyone, especially one aware of his or her divine relationship to the Father, feel unworthy? The secondary fault lies with our conditioning through the years by parents, teachers, ministers, and others who help us form impressions. Too often these contacts speak to us from an error base, a base of misunderstanding of human values. The parents, teachers, ministers, and others who help us form our impressions and who speak from a Truth base are to be desired. They tell us we are worthy, we are loved, we deserve our good. But, for those who feel unworthy, what is the primary fault? It is clearly the acceptance of such ideas as unworthiness and undeserving. It is a personal thing. No outside voice can be blamed. In each of us there is a still, small voice, that tells us the truth—that we are deserving, we are worthy. All too many people refuse to heed this voice; therefore, they plod through life, often in failure, and almost always without peace of mind.

It has been said that there can never be peace in the world as long as men and women engage in civil war with themselves. There also can be little or no peace of mind when we wage war within ourselves.

The still, small voice within has been called "the secret whisper." It calls for us to be our best, to bring forth good in the world, to work for and to establish peace. There is, however, another voice within, "the raucous roar." It calls for us to be negative, to gossip and be petty, to divide rather than unite. Too often it overpowers our still, small voice, our secret whisper, and has its ugly way in our lives. When we yield to the raucous roar, we lead lives as described by Thoreau, "of quiet desperation." There is no peace of mind.

What can silence the raucous roar? Silence is the best tool. Noise of any kind is subservient to quiet. We live in a naturally quiet world. Most of the noise in the world is artificial, unnatural, usually manmade. Stillness is the truth. Noise is a fact. One is normal. The other is abnormal. When the raucous roar within tries to overpower us with force, our disarming mechanism is our ability to become still, to quiet the mind, to curb all unruly emotions and feelings, and to say no to all else but peace. The raucous roar does not like silence. It cannot tolerate a quiet mind. Thus, when you still yourself, it retreats into the netherlands from whence it came.

To some, the idea of stillness, of silence, seems impossible. The raucous roar has its way in their lives, and peace of mind is a casualty. Turmoil reigns in conscious and unconscious activities. There is a solution to this problem just as surely as there is a solution within every problem. It lies in the words of Jesus Christ: *"Let what you say be simply 'yes' or 'no'; anything more than this comes of evil"* (Mt. 5:37).

This beautiful quote from Jesus means exactly what it says, no more and no less. Do not say maybe to peace, or to any other good that you desire. Say yes! Do not say maybe to any negative quality that would try to inhabit your being. Say no! Waffling, or indecisiveness, never brings peace of mind. It always "comes of evil," or brings to you that which you do not want.

When the raucous roar tries to dominate your

thoughts and actions, say no. Say it gently but say it firmly. Immediately replace the raucous roar with a thought or an expression of peace. Jesus taught this two thousand years ago with His powerful demonstration of stilling the storm. *"And he awoke and rebuked the wind, and said to the sea, 'Peace! Be still!' And the wind ceased, and there was a great calm"* (Mk. 4:39).

Peace of mind results when one stills the stormy seas of the mind. It is not easy, this taming of the mind, but it can be done. For many, the idea of positive thinking is new. Time is necessary to change that which time has helped to cement. Our minds did not become tangled in a web of negativity overnight. They cannot become cleared overnight either. Patience is required. The persistent person who works with Truth and holds positive thoughts will be rewarded with measurable degrees of peace of mind over a period of time. Rushing restoration of control over the mind can cause even more inner conflict. Impatience in this respect is akin to the story of the pharoah and Moses in the book of Exodus in the Old Testament. Pharoah's heart was hardened, we are told, and he refused to let the children of Israel go. When we give up too soon in the quest for peace of mind, our hearts are often hardened against trying again. Peace of mind is our most valuable asset. Nothing should stop us short in our pursuit of attaining and keeping it once it is achieved. We must believe. The desire for a peaceful mind cannot be fulfilled without a strong, unwavering belief system. Many people give up too soon. They try to still the raucous roar but their efforts fall short, sometimes just short of success.

Jesus once told a story that makes it clear that peace of mind is the most desirable of all assets. *"The kingdom of heaven* (peace and harmony) *is like a merchant in search of fine pearls, who, on finding one pearl of great value, went and sold all that he had and bought it"* (Mt. 13:45, 46).

What is the *pearl of great value*? There is no doubt that it is peace of mind.

Good health is impossible without peace of mind.

Prosperity is improbable without peace of mind.

Without peace of mind, any good thing that you might have in your life is lessened.

With peace of mind, the door to all good is wide open to each of us.

It behooves us to get on with the job of transforming misunderstanding into understanding and to pay everything we have, and give everything we have, and do all the mental, physical, and emotional work necessary to achieve the pearl of great value, peace of mind.

Part Two

Promises to Keep

Good Health

"Bless the Lord, O my soul . . . who satisfies you with good as long as you live so that your youth is renewed like the eagle's" (Ps. 103:2-5).

*T*he Bible is filled with promises. For those who keep God first in their lives and those who follow the teachings of Jesus Christ each promise is assured. Indeed, those who walk in the light of

God are *"Children of promise"* (Gal. 4:28).

One of the primary Bible promises to each of us as children of God is the one that begins this chapter. No matter how far we have plunged into sickness or disease, it is never too late for our health to be renewed with strength and vitality *like the eagle's*. This is a promise to us. When we do our part, the promise is alive and well. God always does His part.

Regrettably, uncertainty in this respect often leads to loss of peace of mind or failure to attain it in the first place. We simply do not trust God's promises. Oh, we want to believe. We want to trust. But we fail to do so. In fact, we often find it easier to believe for someone else. At times, we can hold the Truth for a sick friend, a child, a parent far easier than we can for ourselves. We can see healing instead of disease, life instead of death. But when we are stricken, often we grin and bear it. We put up with it. We fail to pray the affirmative and positive prayers we are quick to bestow upon another. As a result, our peace of mind suffers. Worry replaces the affirmations that would lead us out of bondage to "dis-ease." Expecting the worst replaces the denials that are vital to an improved condition. We begin to see ourselves as the exception to the law of renewal. But there are no exceptions. Simply turning disbelief into belief puts all the energy of the universe at work on our behalf. Praying with belief, with expectancy, makes all the difference. Myrtle Fillmore, co-founder of Unity, recognized this many, many years ago. Once she did, her life was never the same again.

In 1886 Mrs. Fillmore found herself on the brink of death. Her life flow was quickly ebbing. No medical remedy seemed to help her. No amount of prayer by others on her behalf or by herself on her own behalf seemed to help. She sought everywhere in the outer for relief from a death sentence given to her by medical doctors. Tuberculosis was the verdict. Death was near, the doctors said.

But death sentences are almost always incorrect in the face of a mighty faith that encourages one to persevere and overcome any obstacle. Such was Mrs. Fillmore's faith. Finally she directed it inwardly where Truth dwells. She turned away from doctors, from death sentences, from the "reality" of tuberculosis, and she made a discovery. It rocked her to her very depths of being. It changed her life and indirectly changed thousands, perhaps millions of lives in time to come. Her discovery renewed her life *like the eagle's* and she lived for nearly fifty years more, and with her husband, Charles, founded the great movement known as Unity School of Christianity.

What was Myrtle Fillmore's discovery? It was this: *"Life is simply a form of energy, and has to be guided and directed in man's body by his intelligence. How do we communicate intelligence? By thinking and talking, of course. Then it flashed upon me that I might talk to the life in every part of my body and have it do just what I wanted. I began to teach my body and got marvelous results."*

Was this a miracle? Not at all. It was a realization of Truth, but it was not just a realization of Truth for Mrs. Fillmore. It is for each of us. Mrs. Fillmore did the work. We can use the blueprint she drew for us to work out our particular health challenges. If we do so, our peace of mind grows stronger, our will to live increases, and our joy of life is abundantly magnified.

Mrs. Fillmore talked to her body. She loved the organs that were failing her, she encouraged the blood that coursed through her veins and arteries to do its perfect job in cleansing impurities from her lungs and heart and tissues. She no longer saw her body as diseased and helpless, but as healthy and vital. In the face of facts which cried out death she affirmed the Truth of life. She never looked back after the healing was complete, until in an advanced age by human standards, she simply said goodbye to her friends and family, after this life's work was completed, and made a peaceful transition to another job that she declared awaited her on the other side. She was 86. Her life was and is a shining example to us all.

There are countless examples of such overcomings in the history of the Unity movement, as reported in *Unity* magazine over a 100-year period. "Prayer Power" reports monthly on healings that seem to surpass all understanding. The term *seem* is used advisedly. For you see, appearances can be deceiving. What looks to be impossible to the human mind is routine for God! No appearance of sickness is beyond the healing power of God.

In 1983, the last full year I served as editor-in-chief of Unity School of Christianity, "Prayer Power" recorded personal testimonies of healing of kidney failure, brain tumor, blindness, depression, diabetes, lung cancer, polyps on the cervix, a crippling leg disability, throat cancer, a body crushed in an automobile accident, fluid in the lungs and heart wall, Reye's syndrome, stroke, premature birth complications, and gangrene, to mention just a few of the challenges that were overcome by prayer. Silent Unity, the prayer power arm of Unity School, had prayed with the people facing these challenges. Silent Unity held to the Truth and encouraged those who wrote and called to hold to the Truth in each situation. Results were achieved. Why? Belief! Silent Unity believes in the power of prayer and the power of affirmations and denials. It helps others to believe, also.

Is every physical health challenge subject to healing? Yes. Are all physical challenges healed? No. Therein lies a dilemma. God seems capricious. God seems to bestow healing on one person and permits another to linger in sickness or in a state of disability. One person, who by worldly standards seems undeserving, is healed. Another, a saint by appearances, is not healed. Why is this?

Can we suffice it to say that God knows best, that we do not know as much as God knows and we cannot see what God can see and know?

When we wonder why healing comes to one and not to another, perhaps we should be reminded of the words of Jesus Christ: *"I have yet many things to say to you, but you cannot bear them now"* (Jn. 16:12).

One thing that perhaps Jesus could not tell the people when He lived and walked on the earth and taught the good that He taught was this: sometimes we must be an example for others in *enduring* pain and suffering.

Someone has said that our loss of peace of mind is not necessarily because of disease or sickness or disability, it is because we cannot endure disease or sickness or disability.

Surely you know living examples of this Truth.

A blind woman overcomes her disability by learning to live with it. She becomes proficient at braille. She stays active socially, in her community's affairs, in her church. She compensates for the loss of one sense by cultivating other senses. Her hearing, feeling, and, yes, even her extrasensory perception are enhanced. She learns to live with what the world calls a disability, and in doing so overcomes it!

A person is given a death sentence by a doctor who doesn't understand things of Spirit. The person replies, in effect, "I will die when I decide to die. As for now, I choose to live." By prayer, affirmation, denial, positive thinking, the death sentence is commuted, postponed indefinitely.

A child hears the sad news that a beloved parent is about to die. The parent believes in the death sentence and accepts it. The child does not. The child holds to the Truth, and in the face of such faith, the parent recovers. The child modestly remarks, "He forgot God, and I remembered for him."

Each of us has heard of situations such as these. Sometimes there is a wonderful healing in the physical. Sometimes the healing is at an emotional level. Sometimes the healing is strictly at a spiritual level. But there is always a healing when there is belief, and faith, and love, and the remembrance of God and His will of absolute good for us.

James Dillet Freeman, in an article that first appeared in *Daily Word*, and later in pamphlet form, said that Aristotle was correct in his analysis of the way things happen in this world. Every event has four causes: the material cause, the efficient cause, the formal cause, and the final cause. Let's look at Aristotle's ideas, and Mr. Freeman's conclusions:

The material cause of a house, Mr. Freeman declares, might be thought of as the materials such as nails and lumber.

The efficient cause is a carpenter putting the materials together.

The formal cause is the blueprints an architect prepared.

The final cause is someone's need for shelter.

All four causes are necessary or no house is built. It also follows, Mr. Freeman decided, that all four causes are necessary for either health or sickness.

In sickness, the first (natural) cause is a medical diagnosis. Then, the doctor gives what he or she considers a reason for the diagnosis (efficient cause). The third cause, the formal cause, is our belief in the diagnosis; and the fourth cause, the final cause, is our *acceptance* of the diagnosis.

Causes one and two, material and efficient causes, are purely physical. Causes three and four are *metaphysical*.

It is a matter of science when the doctor tells us we are sick, and why we are sick. It is a matter of Spirit when we decide to believe and/or accept the doctor's verdict.

In a wonderful dissertation on health and sickness, Mr. Freeman says: *"People get sick because they think sickness, accept the possibility of sickness, and carry around the form of sickness, as it were, in their minds."*

If we get sick, it follows that we must do so for a reason, just as there is a reason for the construction of a house. By the same token, if we are well, there must be a reason for our wellness. Thus, the final cuase for both sickness and health is reason. There is a reason for both conditions, and we do not always consciously know the reason.

We can know this: the final cause always includes God. God is a part of everything, both sickness and health, and all other such contrasts. God knows our soul needs. If it should be for our highest good not to demonstrate at a high level of physical expression, God knows the reasons why. Somehow, at a soul level, we must come to understand these hidden reasons. If we do, we will know that even if we do not demonstrate good health physically, we can overcome at an emotional or spiritual level. Working with God, our overcoming is a certainty. It just may not be where we expect it to be.

Our peace of mind, the peace of mind of our families and friends, and all those with whom we come into contact is at stake in this broad concept of sickness or health. First we pray for wholeness, then we pray for "Thy will be done," then we accept that which is ours to work with and overcome at some level of our being, whether it is in the physical, the emotional, or the spiritual. It is so. It cannot be otherwise. For it is as Jesus told us: *"I have yet many things to say to you, but you cannot bear them now."*

Jesus knew that the developing souls of two thousand years ago might not understand many things, suffering and pain among them. But that was then. Now is the time at hand. Our advancement, our evolution as spiritual beings, far exceeds the understanding of that time.

We have come up to here! A very high place in consciousness. We now can bear sickness and pain and suffering when we know it is necessary for our soul's growth. And we can rejoice when the suffering and pain and sickness are eliminated. We are in a pivotal stage of our development as human and as spiritual beings. Acceptance of conditions on occasions that we find unpleasant, and learning to overcome them at *any level* of our being, is vital to peace of mind.

Thus it is that we can affirm perfect health, and more often than not, working with God, achieve it. But, when we do not achieve it at the level expected, we understand and are peaceful.

It is time for us to grow up. It is time for us to mature spiritually, emotionally, physically.

The blind can be healed. Healing is not always a certainty.

The deaf can be healed. Healing is not always a certainty.

The crippled can walk again. Healing is not always a certainty.

The sick can be healed. Healing is not always a certainty.

Our thoughts of absolute and certain healing in every physical situation are thoughts that we should let go. At times something is taking place that is beyond our human ability to understand.

At times healing in the physical simply will not take place no matter how much we pray, or how much anyone prays, or how much we want or anyone else wants the healing to take place.

The success of Silent Unity through almost 100 years of activity in prayer is based on one premise. It is not on healing, not on prosperity, not on spiritual understanding, yet all these are a part of the process. The success of Silent Unity, and the success of the Truth movement in general, is based on one thing only: the highest good of all involved.

God is in charge. He knows our highest good in terms of health, and in terms of every human condition.

But, you say, doesn't this go against the idea of believing and the idea of expectation? No, it does not. It supports it completely.

Believe that you can be healed. This is the foundation of healing. Yes, expect a healing. Without expectation, a healing is not likely to occur. But while you are believing and expecting make the best of whatever situation your consciousness has attracted to you.

Helen Keller did.

Franklin Delano Roosevelt did.

Charles Fillmore did. Although he never completely overcame a disabling injury from his youth, which left one leg shorter by several inches than the other, he improved his physical condition. He was victorious emotionally, spiritually, and ultimately even physically to a large extent.

This saying is so trite, yet so true: when life gives you lemons, make lemonade.

Your physical condition, although subject to perfection, need not hold you back from emotional, spiritual, and physical overcomings.

If you cannot, by prayer and meditation and affirmation and denial, overcome a physical condition, rest assured. God means it for good. Do what you can do and do it to the best of your ability and to the glory of God. It is so. It cannot be otherwise.

Promises to Keep

Prosperity

"Do you not say, 'There are yet four months, then comes the harvest'? I tell you, lift up your eyes, and see how the fields are already ripe for harvest" (Jn. 4:35).

No promise in the Bible is spoken with more authority than this one by Jesus Christ, and it concerns prosperity! Once we plant seeds for spiritual growth and prosperity, reaping can take place immediately. How can we do this? By seeing beyond appearances of lack, by seeing fields white for harvest when in fact the fields are not ready for harvesting. A special something takes place when we deal with things of Spirit that cannot be explained by human or physical logic.

Spirit supersedes all else.

Unity teaches prosperity. It always has and always will. To be prosperous is natural for a child of a King, and God, the true King, desires for His children to be prosperous. If we are not, the fault lies with us and not with the Father. God's flow of good to His children is perpetual. Our receptivity to the good is often blocked by false thinking and negative emotions.

In the early days of the formation of what is now Unity School of Christianity, the founders, Charles and Myrtle Fillmore, came to the awareness that the teaching of prosperity would be a cornerstone of the movement. Not *the* cornerstone. A cornerstone. What a decision that was! Oh, it was unpopular then with some other religious organizations, and still is, but prosperity was Truth then, and it is today. Both of the Fillmores, and every good Unity teacher since their time, envisioned God as a rich Father. In 1892, in their famous covenant, they dedicated their time, money, and all they had to Truth and Unity. All they asked in return was an equivalent in peace of mind, and all the good things that go along with it—health, wisdom, understanding, love, life, and abundant supply. They did their part; God did His.

The Fillmores did not back into prosperity. They achieved it for themselves, for the school they founded, and for the followers in the movement. They went forward into prosperity. So must we. Yet they never made the accumulation of wealth and riches an objective in their lives. Neither should we.

What they did, and we can learn from their example, is to seek the pearl we mentioned earlier, the pearl of great value. They sought peace of mind with all their hearts, minds, and souls and they found it. So can we. Then all things, including prosperity, are at our doorstep.

This is important to remember: the fact that prosperity is literally at our doorstep does not assure it in our lives. We must claim it; we must accept it. Then we must use the prosperity in the highest and best manner.

One of the best examples of why a person does not achieve the objective of prosperity comes from a cartoon that appeared in a magazine some years ago. Here's the scenario: There is a man imploring god, "Please let me win the lottery!" From the clouds above comes a booming voice, presumably God, and He declares: "At least buy a ticket!" Therein lies the problem. Too many people want prosperity, but they are unwilling to pay the price. What is the price? Sharing, giving, loving, caring. Prosperity works two ways. It must flow in and flow out, just as any body of water does if it is to remain fresh and clean. If a body of water only receives, stagnation results. The Dead Sea falls into this category. It only receives. It does not have an outlet. We are like this in terms of prosperity. Unless we learn to give, we cannot receive as we would wish to receive. The *giving* is buying the ticket.

Do you have your ticket? You must have a ticket to ride the prosperity express.

There are, in this nation, people who give a tenth to the source of their good. They are invariably prosperous. There are other people who have a "dollar-bill" consciousness. They are invariably in one degree or another of lack, even of poverty. In between these two peoples are those who give a little more than the dollar and those who give close to the tenth. In each situation, these people have purchased a ticket. Their return is equivalent to their degree of giving. There are few exceptions to the law Jesus Christ gave us: *"Give, and it will be given to you; good measure, pressed down, shaken together, running over, will be put into your lap. For the measure you give will be the measure you get back"* (Lk. 6:38).

For some reason that defies all logic, material or physical, some folks think this is a law for others. It is not a law. It is a promise. The promise is simple: you must give if you wish to receive.

As a minister, I have never met a tithing person who was in poverty. Likewise, I have never met a person in poverty who tithed regularly. It is virtually a certainty that other Unity ministers have encountered this same Truth. When I have said this to non-tithers, the answer has invariably been the same: "But they have money. They can afford to tithe." It doesn't work this way. They tithe, so they can *more* afford to give their tenth.

The truth is that tithing, giving, sharing lead to even more prosperity for the individual who participates in the process. To whom should you give? To the source of your spiritual good. It might be your church; it might be Unity School of Christianity; it might be both, and other such institutions that assist you in your spiritual growth. But wherever you give, give in the right spirit. Never give to lack; give to plenty. Never give from lack; give from plenty. Even if you do not think you have plenty, affirm that it is from plenty that you give. This cannot be emphasized too much. You are a rich child of a rich Father. When you accept this idea and begin to live it totally, in mind and in action, it will become true for you even if it is not a fact.

If you are new to Truth, and are from an orthodox background, be careful of the prosperity-poverty trap. It is a simple one, but one that has caused thousands, maybe millions, to believe that it is our destiny to suffer, to have lack, in this lifetime, so that reward might come later, in heaven. Heaven cannot be put off. Heaven is right now, when we are in the right frame of mind, when we are in harmony with life and with God. There is nothing wrong with having money. Jesus Christ taught prosperity. Prosperity is biblical. Do not listen to anyone, no matter what his credentials might be, who says that it is a virtue to be poor. Charles Fillmore once said that it is a sin to be poor. He knew, of course, that sin is a mistake. What he meant was, it is a mistake to be poor.

This book is about the peace that passes all misunderstanding. One of the greatest misunderstandings in orthodox Christianity is that money is the root of all evil. Paul did not say this. What he said was: *"For the love of money is the root of all evils"* (I Tim. 6:10). *The love of* money is not spiritual. There is no reason to love money. What we need to do, for the sake of our peace of mind and our spiritual understanding, is to appreciate and be grateful for money and all that it represents. Money is not dirty or ugly. Money is a symbol of substance. It is good. When we love it, we diminish its power to do for us what Spirit would have it do in our lives. When we respect its source, and are grateful for it, we use it wisely, and we share it and keep it in circulation. To say that money is evil is akin to saying air is evil because, if it is misused, it is dangerous. Water, if misused, is dangerous. Fire, if misused, is dangerous. Money, in its right relationship with humankind is a beautiful tool for good. So get it out of your mind right now, if you suffer from the delusion that poverty is spiritual. Money keeps our world in operation. Without it our world would stagnate. Without money you would be dependent on the society in which you live. You would be without power in daily activities. God would not want His children to be without the means of participating fully in the society in which they live.

Myrtle Fillmore said it beautifully many years ago: *"Money is all right. It serves us splendidly if we know how to use it."* And George Bernard Shaw added: *"The lack of money is the root of all evil."* Shaw went on to make this profound statement: *"Money is the most important thing in the world. It represents health, strength, honor, generosity, and beauty as conspiculously as the want of it represents illness, weakness, disgrace, meanness, and ugliness. The greatest of all evils and the worst of crimes is poverty. All other crimes are virtues beside it. Poverty spreads horrible pestilence, and strikes at the souls of those who come within sight, sound, or smell of it."*

Perhaps we should not go quite as far as Mr. Shaw. But he is more right than wrong. Each of us is a child of the Father. No child of a rich Father has the right to rejoice in poverty. We should rejoice in prosperity.

What do others say of money?

"Money is like muck, not good except it be spread."—Francis Bacon.

"Poverty is the most deadly and prevalent of all diseases."—Eugene O'Neill.

"For to him who has will more be given, and he will have abundance; but from him who has not, even what he has will be taken away"— Jesus Christ (Mt. 13:12).

Who do you believe? Those who say poverty is a virtue or those who say prosperity is the way of life? When Jesus Christ told us those who have will receive more, and for those who have not, even that which they have will be taken away, what could He have meant?

The answer follows logically and naturally in the book of Matthew, verses 18 through 23, where Jesus tells of the parable of the sower.

That which you have must be sown in good soil, not in thorns (sense gratification, extravagance), not on rocky ground (useless and unnecessary spending), but that which you have should be used for the good of all. After the good that your consciousness attracts to you meets your needs, your family's needs, sharing with others is necessary. First and foremost you need to share with your spiritual source of good.

Jesus taught us, so beautifully: *"As for what was sown on good soil, this is he who hears the word and understands it; he indeed bears fruit"* (Mt. 13:23).

Let us finish this study of prosperity, and your right to enjoy it and share it with others, with these suggestions.

If you want to be prosperous, and you are not now experiencing this God-given right:

Keep God first in your life.

Follow the teachings of Jesus Christ to the best of your ability.

Do not hoard or foolishly use your money.

Do not possess money or let it possess you. Use it.

If you save it, do it for logical, spiritual reasons. Do not prepare for a rainy day. You will get rained on.

Bless all that you have and all that you want to receive.

Give, give, give, all that you can to the source of your spiritual good.

Do not believe in debt or you will go into it.

Never see lack. See abundance.

Never envy anyone with more than you have.

Live a life of simplicity, but enjoy a luxury from

time to time. You are a child of God. You deserve it.

Above all, know that prosperity is spiritual, and that you deserve all the good that the universe has to offer you. Claim it. Be peaceful about your good.

Promises to Keep

Spiritual Illumination

"And you will know the truth, and the truth will make you free" (Jn. 8:32).

No promise in the Bible is more rewarding to the person who understands this quote from John.

The three major components in every Silent Unity prayer session are the divine ideas of health, prosperity, and spiritual illumination (or spiritual understanding). In the two preceding chapters, health and prosperity were discussed from a standpoint of peace of mind. Health and prosperity are vital for one's peace of mind, but spiritual illumination is even more essential.

Just what did Jesus mean when He said that

we will know the truth and it will make us free? This question has perplexed people for almost 2,000 years. What is truth? Pilate asked Jesus this question in the book of John. There is no record of an answer. Did Jesus stand mute? Or did He answer and His remark was felt to be insignificant or irrelevant? We do not know and it does no good to conjecture. But it does do some good to think spiritually about the possible response to the quesiton. Charles Fillmore did just this. His conclusion, found in *The Revealing Word*, is:

"Truth is the absolute; that which accords with God as divine principle; that which is, has been, and ever will be; that which eternally is."
This is about as good an answer as anyone will give to this puzzling question of What is Truth? But is Mr. Fillmore's answer fully understandable? From a physical, mental, human standpoint, we must respond, no. The answer will always be no from a physical, mental, human standpoint. We can never fully understand spiritual truth from a physical, mental, human standpoint. To try to do so is a means of destroying peace of mind. Paul taught us this in his first letter to the Corinthians. His message was simple: spiritual things must be discerned spiritually. He said: *"The unspiritual* (or natural) *man does not receive the gifts of the Spirit of God, for they are*

folly to him, and he is not able to understand them because they are (or must be) *spiritually discerned''* (1 Cor. 2:14).

To repeat: We wreck our peace of mind when we try to understand at a human level things that are wholly of Spirit. We must come to an understanding that *we do not need to understand everything*. In fact, complete understanding of everything would not be for our highest good. It would take all the zest and mystique out of life.

A spiritually based person knows he does not need to understand things of Spirit. A spiritually based person knows that faith transcends the need to know, the need to understand. In effect, spiritual illumination is anything but physical knowing. It is intuitive knowing.

Take the most basic Unity teaching, that of God's nature of absolute good. Can we *know* this intellectually? Oh, we might say we can. But there will be times when we will waver. How can we know that God is absolute good? Only by intuitive knowing, by spiritual knowing, by faith. There is no way that we can prove God as absolute good when we use intellectual reasoning. Spiritual things must be discerned spiritually. Spiritual truth cannot be proved by intellectual means. But, when we try to prove Spirit by spiritual methods, we achieve our objective. When we ask God His nature, in prayer, and then listen peacefully, spiritually, the answer comes to us as clearly as if written on stone: *I AM good*. We cannot use this means to prove God's nature to another human being. We can explain our method, of course, and another may try our method or some variation of it, but each person's answer must come from within. Then, and only then, is the proof established.

Human beings are naturally inquisitive. We want to know what, where, when, who, why, and how. Our first major question in life might well be *why*? At first the human response is *why*. Then, soon, regrettably in all too many situations, it becomes *why me*? Why seems natural. We want to understand. As children we want to understand why we cannot climb too high, dig too deep, stray too far from the confines of our neighborhoods. We ask probing questions of those who care for us. Why am I here? Why am I in this life situation? Why? Why? Why? As we are exposed to things of Spirit it naturally follows that we ask Spirit why. But this is intellectual questioning and it has its limits. When that limit is reached, and it surely must vary from human to human, peace of mind is at stake if we attempt to go beyond it. It is precisely at this point that spiritual questions must be asked and answers sought. We must stop, at some point, our intellectual pursuit of knowledge of things of

Spirit. Our peace of mind is at stake.

Understanding of human situations is to be desired. It is good for our souls to seek intellectual understanding in human situations. Even there, there may be a limit. There, too, we may need to discern spiritually. There is never a time when spiritual discernment is wrong.

Something that may challenge your understanding at this very point is the idea, common in Truth circles, that each of us already knows everything there is to know. Do you believe this? The Fillmores did. It is almost certain Jesus Christ did, although He never told us this in so many words. In Truth, it is believed that within us is all that there is, in potential. As we unfold this inner potential, knowledge comes to the surface. In other words, when you learn something from a teacher, or a book, or some other means, you are really only recognizing something that is already within you but which has not until this time revealed itself to you.

This phenomenon is readily apparent to one who has been raised in an orthodox religious background and suddenly finds a Unity church, or some other Truth organization such as Unity School of Christianity. What such a person hears or reads is exactly right. "Why, I have always believed this way," is a common expression. When it is discovered that others also have such beliefs, permission is granted, so to speak, for these buried beliefs to come forth.

Just as it works in this manner for things of Spirit, so does it work with mathematics, languages, chemistry, etc. Each human being is a complete package. We are threefold beings. Our nature is body, soul, Spirit. The Spirit within each of us, the Christ within as it is described in Unity, is perfect, all-knowing. The soul is a combination of all that we are in thought and in feeling, and the body is the wonderful vehicle for the soul and Spirit. In the absolute we know everything and understand everything. At body and soul levels we bring out into the open the hidden potential of the treasure within. The understanding that comes forth is in direct proportion to our soul need at the very time it comes forth. For us to try to force more understanding is to diminish our peace of mind. *Let understanding come forth in its proper time and place*, is a wonderful affirmation for each of us.

Albert Einstein once said true understanding takes place when we know that we do not have to know why or how in every situation but simply trust the intuitive mind. The deep level of Einstein's spiritual understanding is often overshadowed by his intellectual understanding. We could learn much from him from both levels. Once, at a meeting in which he was in the audience, a remark was made that stirred Einstein to rise to his feet and declare: "Yes, that is true. It must be so! God could not have made it different." After the meeting he went to his laboratory and proved the speaker, himself, and God to be correct.

"It must be so! God could not have made it different," is not intellectual understanding. It is spiritual, intuitive understanding. And it is the very best kind. At times it can even be proved intellectually, as Einstein did, but it is never necessary. Things of Spirit need not be proved intellectually.

Einstein was well read, naturally. Perhaps you are, too. But Jesus Christ was not. There is no evidence that He ever read anything other than the ancient Scriptures that we now call the Old Testament. Much of His understanding came from these Scriptures. Where did the rest of it come from? From God is the easy answer. From the voice of God within is the right answer. The God that indwelled Jesus permitted Him to say such a thing as:

"Do you not believe that I am in the Father and the Father in me? The words that I say to you I do not speak on my own authority; but the Father who dwells in me does his works" (Jn. 14:10).

You are in the Father and the Father is in you.

When you listen to the still voice of the Christ within, you too will speak with authority higher than your own. Spiritual illumination in you will be a living, breathing part of you, and understanding will be your true nature.

Charles Fillmore said there are two ways to get understanding: *"One is by following the guidance of Spirit that dwells within; and the other is to go blindly ahead and learn by hard experience."*

Too many of us are trying the latter course. It does our peace of mind great damage. It follows logically, and spiritually, that intuitive knowing far exceeds any other kind of knowledge.

If you love nature, and every child of God should, consider this: As you walk about examining the beautiful trees and plants and flowers, and see the little creatures scampering about, the butterflies and birds on their flights of fancy, taste the fresh air, breathe it deeply, is there a need to physically understand all this? Of course not. The only need is to be grateful to the Source of all this good and beauty in our lives. Gratitude can almost always eliminate our need to know, to understand, at a physical level.

In one of the greatest demonstrations of pure spiritual understanding, spiritual illumination, Myrtle Fillmore, writing in *How to Let God Help You*, a Unity book, said:

"If you would grow in understanding of spiritual things, become as a little child and let the universal spirit of good teach you. Do not strain your intellect in trying to understand the mighty questions of life; wait until you have developed faculties which can comprehend them. There is a running to and fro among men that will never cease so long as they try to explain spiritual things with intellect. Listen to the stillness within your own soul—and you will find it resonant with a new tongue."

Now do you understand? Your peace of mind requires that you understand that you do not need to understand everything intellectually, but that you *can* understand everything spiritually, if you listen to the voice of God within you.

Perfect peace of mind results when the latter course is followed.

Promises to Keep

The Bible

"All scripture is inspired by God and profitable for teaching, for reproof, for correction, and for training in righteousness, that the man of God may be complete, equipped for every good work" (2 Tim. 3:16, 17).

Somehow, in the time since Paul lived and wrote these words, orthodox Christianity came to the conclusion that what Paul really meant was that the Bible is the absolute inerrant work of God. Wrong. Paul never said this. Neither did Jesus. First of all, there was no Bible when these two spiritual giants lived. There were only the sacred writings that we now call the Old Testament. Jesus knew nothing of the New Testament.

He, to our knowledge, never wrote a word for the printed page. Paul also did not write with the conscious knowledge that he was creating scripture. Paul was writing letters, letters to friends, letters to churches. It was not for centuries that his letters became scripture. Neither Paul nor Jesus knew they were helping build a New Testament. What they both tried to do, Jesus through speaking and Paul through speaking and writing, was to build a new way of life for people to follow. They knew that if they were successful, those to follow would have peace of mind, or dwell in heaven.

The Bible is a source of great comfort and joy to millions of people. To millions of other people it is a book of torture, death, pain, suffering, sin, disappointment, confusion, and they refuse to enter into communion with it.

The Bible is a book of promise and it is a book of despair, and the difference between the two views is simply a matter of perspective. It is unquestionably the largest selling and most-printed book in the world. Yet, most Bibles gather dust and are rarely opened except for family entries such as births and deaths. It is ridiculed; it is praised. It brings laughter to some, tears to others. It is revered and scorned. It is said to be inerrant by fundamentalists and a hoax and a fraud by atheists. Some see it as a book of life, others as a book of death.

Whatever the Bible is, it is this: It is a book that can help you find peace of mind, or lose it. It is all in your perspective. Read the Bible with metaphysical interpretation and understanding, and you will be at peace. Read it literally, and inner conflict is sure to take place. This is why Unity has for some 100 years interpreted the Bible. Charles Fillmore has said, in *The Revealing Word:* "*A spiritual interpretation of the Bible demands that the meaning of every figure, type, parable, and symbol must be in harmony with the fundamental principles of Being.*" He adds: "*The Bible is a recital of what has taken place in the consciousness of man, of the results of his working, either intelligently with the law or unintelligently against it, in seeking his own salvation. It gives an explanation of spiritual law as applied to man and tells him how to find the kingdom of heaven within.*"

This is what the Bible is all about. If you cannot relate to the characters, to the situations, and put yourself in their places, you will not likely gain a great deal from reading the Bible. If you can, great spiritual growth is certain to take place.

The Bible is not inerrant; it is inspired. It was written by inspired men (and very likely some inspired women who did not get the credit), and the inspiration came to them from God. All inspiration comes from the source of all good, God. But, sometimes the channel through which it comes to us can be somewhat clogged by human consciousness.

Years ago, when I was editor in chief of Unity School of Christianity, occasionally someone would submit a poem or essay with the declaration: "God wrote this through me. If you reject it, you are rejecting God." I had to reject God a lot on this basis. But, I was occasionally tempted to ask the writer, in the event I wanted to accept the piece, "Do I send the check to you or to God?" I never yielded to this temptation, but had I done so, I am sure the writer would have wanted the check made out in his or her name. Yet, this person was of a mind that God did the work! God does not do the work. He provides the inspiration. We do the work. Our work, after being filtered through our consciousness, may be very ungodlike, or it may be very godlike. The result is up to us. Our consciousness rules the results.

And so it was with the Bible. These were good men (and/or women) who wrote the Good Book. God did not write it. God inspired it.

Some years ago an atheist got into the news by demanding that the Bible come equipped with a warning label, much like those used in advertisements for cigarettes: *WARNING: Literal belief in this book may endanger your health and life.* This came about after a man took the Bible passage literally about cutting off your hand and gouging out your eye for wrongdoing. Maybe a warning label wouldn't be a bad idea. But a more positive warning label would be more desirable. How about: *Reading this book without wisdom, discernment, and interpretation can lead to loss of peace of mind!*

Yes, there are times to take the Bible literally. There are times to recognize history, mythology, folklore. There are times to interpret.

A missionary once boasted to George Bernard Shaw that he had just returned from Africa where he had "saved" thousands of people and converted them to Christianity. Not only that, but to every person who had been saved, the missionary had given a native-language Bible. "Good heavens," Shaw declared. "Do those people have guns?" Yes, the missionary replied. "Are they good shots?" Yes, the missionary replied. And Shaw shouted, "Don't you know what you have done? Those innocent people will take the Bible literally and when they find out we don't, they will come and shoot us."

Well, maybe it isn't this bad. But the point is well taken. The innocent and naive people on this earth who take the Bible literally often are intolerant of those of us who don't. Their verdict for us is always the same: eternal fire and damnation and suffering. Anyone who takes the Bible literally can be a danger to society and to themselves.

H. L. Mencken has said that the Bible is the most beautiful book ever written. Mencken, a famed editor, says no literature ever produced is a match for it. Abraham Lincoln called it the best gift God has ever given man. On the other hand, Voltaire predicted in the 1700s that within a century the Bible would disappear from the face of the earth.

Despite the assaults on it by a maturing spiritual society, the Bible continues to survive and thrive. It survives in spite of its errors, its inconsistencies, its exaggerations, its weaknesses. It survives because of its Truths, its consistencies, its strengths.

The Old Testament scriptures have been with us for well over 2,000 years. The New Testament has been in its present form more than 1,500 years. A first testament, a second testament. Will there be a third? Controversial as it may seem to some people, it is in the realm of possibility that a third testament will evolve in future years. And perhaps a fourth, and a fifth. The unfolding story of the rise in consciousness of men and women is not finished with the New Testament.

There is more to come, and when it comes, there would be no surprise at all to most practical Christians to find the writings of metaphysical giants. But the Third Testament is still in incubation. If it comes, in another time and place, it will be in divine order.

But, for now, we deal with the two testaments we have. Perhaps we think, why didn't God give us an inerrant book? Why didn't God just put it all down in black and white so we would know exactly what we need to do for our highest good? The only valid answer any thinking person can produce is that God loves us too much to dictate to us. God has given us the valuable gift of choice. We have choices. The Bible, Old and New Testaments, is full of choices.

An absolutely good God, which our God is, would never order His children to think or to act in a certain manner. An absolutely good God would do exactly as God has done for us: He would let us choose. Thank You, Father!

What is the authority of the Bible? The answer is one word. *You* are the authority. No one else. You must read the Bible with an understanding heart and mind, a mind which discerns between that which rings true and that which is false. Do you want to give that right over to another person? Of course not. We have done that for centuries. We have let priests and religious leaders and ministers tell us what to believe and how to respond to life. It is time for us to grow up in this area, too, and accept the responsibility of reading and comprehending and accepting or rejecting the Bible from a personal, yet spiritual, standpoint. Am I calling for selective acceptance of what the Bible tells us. You bet I am. And such acceptance, or rejection, when done on a spiritual basis is the only valid way to read and to interpret the Bible. Of course you may receive guidance from another. A minister might tell you his or her view of a biblical situation. It then is up to you to consider the view presented, and then find it right or wrong for your own personal soul growth.

Perhaps one of the most valuable sets of books ever printed are those written by Elizabeth Sand Turner, (Unity Books) in what is known as the Turner trilogy: *Let There Be Light*, a study of the Old Testament; *Your Hope of Glory*, a study of the Gospels; and *Be Ye Transformed*, a study of Paul's writings, the epistles, and Revelation. A student cannot go wrong with this material, for even if one disagrees with the interpretations Mrs. Turner places on characters and situations, her ideas are thought-provoking and help one come to a personal interpretation.

When all is said and done concerning the Bible, this much is certain: There are many translations and interpretations of the Bible, but the most effective translation and interpretation is in your own life.

As you continue through life you will meet many people who will tell you that if you do not accept the Bible as the inerrant word of God, you are doomed. Do not argue with them. It does no good. But remember this, the Bible is the book of life. It is the book of your life. It is your life that is at stake. If you do not come to an understanding of this, your peace of mind will suffer. If you do understand that you not only have the right, but the duty, to interpret and translate for yourself, you will find peace and happiness.

The Bible can assist you in solving the many challenges we have in life. The characters in the Bible have gone through, and grown through, practically every problem known to humankind. As we read of these overcomings, we are strengthened by the successes. As we read of the apparent failures in the Bible, we are wise to learn the lessons therein.

When you need to feel loved, and there is no one to touch you physically, you may open your Bible to the New Testament and feel the love of Jesus Christ as He says: *"As the Father has loved me, so have I loved you"* (Jn. 15:9).

When you are lonely, and there is no one to comfort you physically, you may open your

Bible to the New Testament and feel the love of Jesus Christ when He says: *"Lo, I am with you always"* (Mt. 28:20).

When you are not at peace, and there is no one nearby to help you, you may open your Bible to the New Testament and become at one with all there is in the words of Jesus Christ when He says: *"Peace I leave with you; my peace I give to you"* (Jn. 14:27).

Can you find help in the Old Testament? Oh, yes, especially in the Psalms. In the Proverbs. Throughout the Old Testament there is help to be found.

Is the Bible outdated? Only if you are.

Is the Bible helpful? Only if you use it correctly.

Is the Bible inspired? Yes, and it can inspire you to new spiritual heights in soul growth.

Happy reading!

Promises to Keep

God and Humanity

"Do you not know that you are God's temple and that God's Spirit dwells in you?" (1 Cor. 3:16).

*W*e have already established the nature of God as absolute good and that God indwells each of us. But for the sake of our peace of mind, we must come to another understanding that is basic equipment for a growing student of Truth. It is simply this: there cannot be, ever, in any way, any separation between God and humanity, *except in our own belief in such separation*. Such belief is in error.

The human belief that God could, or would, or worse yet, even does, turn His back on His children at any time, in any situation, is a cause of great loss in terms of peace of mind. God and we are linked eternally with no possibility of separation of any kind. Coming to this understanding helps assure peace of mind.

Once there was a newspaper editor who sat pondering on the great questions of life as he gazed out a window. Suddenly it occurred to him that it had been cloudy for more than a week. The sun had not peeked through the clouds even once in that time.

"Get me a story on why the sun hasn't been shining for more than a week," he shouted at another editor, who took the assignment to another editor, who finally passed it off on a disbelieving reporter.

"You want me to do what?" he demanded incredulously.

But the reporter did his part. He called all the proper places, the weather bureau, the local university for learned opinions, and he came up with a one-line story after considerable effort. It read: *"The sun isn't shining because the clouds is in the way."*

Ungrammatically, even sarcastically, he made a point. When the sun doesn't shine on us during the day, it is always because the clouds are in the way. Nothing else can keep it from shining on us during daytime hours.

A spiritual analogy concerning the relationship between God and us can be found in this story of the newspaper report. It is, in whole:

God's light does not always seem to shine on us because we block it with our clouds of negative emotions and thoughts.

The clouds obstruct the sun at times. We partially obstruct God's light with negativity. But, no matter how much the clouds might obstruct the sun, it still shines and even through the clouds some of it reaches us. It follows that even through our negativity, some of God's light reaches us. We cannot block it totally, except in our consciousness, our belief system. Still, the light gets through. God goes right on doing His perfect work on our behalf. Nothing can stop His goodness at work in our lives, and even when we *think* we are apart, we cannot be. That which is a part of something can never be apart from that which it is.

God and we are *one*.

The error that there can be a separation between God and us originated in the fable of Adam and Eve and has been perpetuated by zealous church leaders through many centuries.

In the Adam and Eve allegory we have the first two residents of our world listening to the footsteps of God as He walks through His garden. The Genesis account has our two original human

beings hiding from God because they have par-
taken of the forbidden fruit. It further, rather
foolishly but innocently, has God having to ask
them, "Where are you?" Thus, from the very
beginning of the Judeo-Christian tradition we
gave God human characteristics and qualities. It
was possible to hear His voice, hear His
footsteps, even to look upon Him and talk to
Him as one human talks to another. It was possible to hide from Him and to force Him to ask
our whereabouts. From the very beginning that
which was unlimited was sorely limited. The idea
of separation of God and humanity was born
when, in the Genesis allegory, God sent Adam
and Eve into the wilderness. It might be said that
we have wandered in the wilderness of sense ever
since. Especially in terms of believing in the possibility of enmity and separation.

In order to come to terms with peace of mind
concerning God and ourselves, the first consideration must be this: God does not punish us
for our sins; we are punished *by* them. How
much better the allegory in Genesis of Adam and
Eve would have served us if this truth had been
demonstrated and expressed.

It was up to Jesus Christ to reveal the truth
about God to us, and He did so with His words:
*"God is spirit, and those who worship him must
worship in spirit and truth"* (Jn. 4:24). God is

not human. That image of God is utterly limiting. God is spirit. That image of Him is totally freeing. Our coming to this understanding is vital to our peace of mind.

The relationship between God and any other person on this globe is none of your spiritual business. Your relationship with God is 100 percent your spiritual business. It is vital that you do not depend on any other human being in seeking a personal relationship with God. You might get help from many other people, but be a disciple of no one. Depend only on the Christ within as you seek such a relationship.

As you work with Spirit to come to a spiritual understanding of your nature and the nature of God, you will, if you are in earnest, come to these understandings concerning yourself:

You are a divine idea and you exist because God thought you into existence.

You are created in God's image and likeness. The true you exists within the physical you. You are far more than flesh and blood, which you seem to be; in truth, you are pure Spirit. This is the image of God as you.

You are perfect, as God is perfect, at the spirit level, and your very reason for being in this incarnation is to bring the physical up to the spiritual level of being. With each thought, with each action, your every ideal should include the transformation from the human to the spiritual level.

By your thoughts and actions you create the world in which you live. If you think wisdom, there is wisdom. If you think misunderstanding, there is misunderstanding. The world, the true world, is a world built on thought. If you have thought your world into lack and sickness and misunderstanding, you can rethink it into the opposites of plenty and health and understanding. God's one mind is linked to all human minds. God is constantly transmitting elevating thoughts to us. When our receiver is clear of negativity, we truly understand and act accordingly.

You are not limited. Threescore and ten is a lie. You cannot do this or that is a lie. You are God in action when you act properly on God-thought, and you are totally unlimited.

You have not been measured and found to fall short. You have been measured for greatness and for divinity. You are great and divine. You need only to intuitively know and live as if you are and you will be in all your ways great and divine.

You, the true you, are immortal. Only the flesh is temporal. What you truly are will live on forever, constantly growing, unfolding, to total oneness with the Father.

You are spiritual, and oh, so very special to God. God needs you as His expression on earth. You are His arms and His legs, and you have much good work to do and much growth to achieve.

You are never alone.

Likewise, as you work with Spirit to come to a spiritual understanding of the nature of God, you will come to these conclusions:

God truly is absolute good. You will know it at a level of feeling that you have never before experienced.

God is the ruler of the universe, and He is a benevolent ruler. There is nothing negative or little or mean in God. To believe such negates the beautiful idea of God as absolute good.

God, although without human characteristics, is as personal to us when we know Him spiritually as our very breath. When we know that He indwells us He becomes for us, in mind and in expression, *totally* personal. Those who want or believe in a God with human features often say Truth takes away the personal God and replaces it with cold, hard principle. The soft, warm principle that indwells you cannot be more personal. Sharing the same life is as personal as personal can be, both physically and spiritually.

God is love. When we come to this understanding and declare our oneness with Him, we also declare we are one in love. Then, in our human expression, we may find it possible to be hateful or spiteful, for we always have choices, but we will find it totally undesirable to demonstrate in such a manner. We find it is not enough to know the Truth. We must also live it. Then our joy is complete.

We come to an understanding that God is accessible, approachable. We can approach God at any time, in any situation and find comfort and peace of mind, and what is best, answers to our needs and wants and questions.

Yes, we come to the understanding that God is all. Nothing else counts quite so much as this knowledge, for even in the face of what appears to be evil, we can be sure that God is a part of whatever is taking place. We can know that in whatever situation we find ourselves, at high or low moments in life, God is there. God's love is there. God's peace is there. We truly are never alone.

All this, and so much more than time and space allow, assures us of our divine relationship with the Father.

Separation between God and humanity is an absurdity and a spiritual impossibility. This knowledge is a basis for peace of mind.

You are God's temple, and God's spirit dwells in you! Be at peace.

Promises to Keep

Jesus Christ

"Truly, truly, I say to you, he who believes in me will also do the works that I do; and greater works than these will he do, because I go to the Father" (Jn. 14:12).

*O*h, what a promise! The plan of salvation? It is nothing compared to this one. Repentance? Oh, yes, it is important that we change our ways and do right. But even repentance pales in comparison to the promise in John 14:12. In the verse that starts this chapter we find the ultimate promise in the teachings of Jesus Christ. It is a promise that traditionalists would have us ignore. Literalists try to explain it away. Fundamentalists say surely Jesus meant something else, which in our human condition we simply cannot understand.

Jesus meant what He said, and in saying what He said, He gave us the key to His life and ministry. He was the first to do great wonders and works because he went to the Father, but He was not the last. We, too, may do all that He did and more, if we follow His way of life, if we, too, go to the Father.

If ever a teaching has been hidden, this is a prime example.

Christianity began with Jesus Christ. He never called it that, and it is seriously to be doubted that He ever intended to found a religion. He intended (it is a virtual certainty) to found a way of life. Paul probably can get most of the credit for Christianity, and in some respects Christianity is more "Paulianity" than it is "Jesusianity." Jesus Christ gave us a way of life. Paul gave us churches and organization and dogma and doctrine. Paul is much to be credited for his zeal in spreading the idea of Christianity; he is, regretfully, not especially to be regarded for the trappings he gave Christianity.

What we are involved in, in our study of Truth, is practical Christianity. Take away all the ritual, all the organization, all the doctrine and dogma, and go back to the original teachings of Jesus Christ, follow them to the best of your ability, and you are a practical Christian. This is Unity—practical, logical, explainable. Truth is simply this: the teachings of Jesus applied in the everyday lives of human beings.

At one level of understanding, Jesus is the son of Mary and Joseph. He is historically accurate. He lived. He taught. He died. He was resurrected into eternal life. Few doubt that He lived. Few doubt that He taught. Few doubt that He died.

The resurrection? That is another story. Some doubt it. The ascension? Some doubt it. Truth students accept it because it is the very basis of all Christianity. Without it, His teachings are not valid. He taught that death could be overcome. He taught that He would do it. Either He did it, and He is a valid teacher, or He did not do it, and He is an invalid teacher. Christianity, the truth of it, is at stake.

Believe He did it. Put all doubts out of your mind. This believing faith will free you. It will allow you to fully understand the quote that opens this chapter. Without belief we will never be able to do the works that He did. And we do want to do them. That much is for sure, if we are earnest students of Truth.

Charles Fillmore, in *The Revealing Word*, calls Jesus Christ the perfect idea of God for us. Jesus is the expression, Mr. Fillmore said, of the divine idea man.

For a moment, let's think of a comic book hero such as Superman or Captain Marvel or Spiderman or whatever other such character that may come to mind. Can we emulate such heroes? Of course not. It is illogical. Superman was born, the story goes, in another galaxy on another planet, and he was a godlike figure with supernatural powers. Captain Marvel, as I recall from my youth, had a formula. He used the magic word, "Shazam," which transformed him into a super hero. (Oh, the little boys, and girls, who have tried shouting Shazam!)

No shout of Shazam has ever turned a child into a Captain Marvel, that is for sure.

So what of Jesus? Is He a superman? Is it possible that He had a secret word? If so, forget it friends, you cannot emulate Him. He is, if this is true, far beyond us in every category that counts. If He is wholly God, there is no hope for us, for we are not wholly god. We are Godlike, but we are very, very human.

Thus the problem: Was Jesus Christ very God?

If He was very God, forget the quote that started this chapter. It is worthless as it concerns us. But what if He was wholly human with a wholly-God potential?

Wait just a minute. That sounds like something we can relate to and understand. In fact, it is the only thing that makes sense.

A person who can fly without the aid of an airplane could not teach us to do so. It is unnatural. In fact, such a person would be unnatural. But a person who can learn the good way to live, the higher path, can very well teach others the way. This is natural. Then, it follows, if such a person can learn of the existence of a higher law, and reveal it to us, then we, too could experience the benefits of that higher law.

Jesus was not God. He was man on His way to becoming fully Godlike, just as each of us is on the same route, each at our own pace and to our own degree of understanding.

Jesus was born, the story goes, in Bethlehem. His mother was Mary. His father was God. Really? Maybe. Probably not. Most likely Joseph was the true Father, and the story of the virgin birth was an exaggeration felt necessary by such writers as the writer of Matthew and Luke. It is interesting to note that the writers of Mark and John felt the story unimportant enough to omit from their gospels. Whether or not you believe in the virgin birth, and it is much in debate, the important thing to think of is this: Jesus must have been fully human or His example for us is worthless. There is no human way a human can emulate a god. There are too many limitations in the human condition.

Charles Fillmore, again in *The Revealing Word*, writes that Jesus had a mission: *"to connect the thinker with the source of thought."* He could not do this without first becoming fully cognizant of His own source, His own natural progression through life.

He must have known His humanness. There are countless evidences to this fact:

He ate and drank. He was accused of gluttony and being a drunkard and a friend of tax collectors and sinners (Mt. 11:19). (Hardly the publicity reserved for that of gods!)

He spoke of having a soul, of it being sorrowful, even to death (Mt. 26:38). Hardly a godlike condition.

He spoke of His utter desolation, His abandonment, from the Cross. He cried out in despair (Mt. 27:46).

He dreaded death. Yet He faced it (Lk. 12:50). Is this the stuff of which gods are made?

Yes. The answer is yes. All these human conditions are prerequisites to godhood. Jesus went through them, and so must we. Jesus was wholly human and He became wholly God. So it is that this is our destiny.

To believe anything less torments our peace of mind. To believe anything else is contrary to what He taught.

Jesus was subject to every human condition.

Indeed, He was subject to far more negative and destructive conditions than most of us will ever face. How many of us are taken to a cross where we are pierced and nailed? Oh, we have our challenges. But few of ours can match His in the human condition.

Yet, through it all, there is the beautiful promise that we can do everything He did, if we go to the Father as He did. And what did He do that we would want to do?

Heal.

Prosper.

Illuminate.

All these and more.

Yes, Jesus allowed Himself to be called the Son of God, for He knew with a knowing that surpasses all human understanding that He was in the process of becoming God. He was living out His divinity. He had lived the human life and had sought for and found the divine life.

What does this teach us? Simply this: that we too are in the process of becoming God. We are living out our divinity. We are living the human life and we are seeking for, and will find, the divine life. How can we be so assured? Because Jesus told us so. Jesus told us, and it is a promise, that everything He did, we can do, *"if we go to the Father."*

Some call Jesus the Annointed.

Some call Him the Messiah.

In Unity, in Truth, we call Him the Way-Shower. He showed us the way to eternal life with the Father. He drew for us a roadmap.

Eric Butterworth has pointed out the folly of "Jesus worship" by writing that Jesus created for us a window to look through in order that we may see the way and the life. Far too many people, Butterworth points out, have mistaken His teachings. Instead of looking through the window, and focusing attention on the way and the life, they have made Jesus an object of worship.

To worship Jesus is an error. To follow His teachings is the way to overcoming. Jesus said as much when He is quoted thus: *"And he said to him, 'Why do you ask me about what is good? One there is who is good. If you would enter life, keep the commandments' "* (Mt. 19:17).

The truth is this: Jesus did not ask to be worshiped. He asked to be followed. He asked us, his younger brothers and sisters, to follow Him. Truly, He is our Elder Brother, and as such, is eager for us to learn the way that He discovered leads to life and complete happiness.

The way you see Jesus Christ makes all the difference in your life, in your spiritual progress, in your peace of mind.

Promises to Keep

The Truth About Age

"They still bring forth fruit in old age, they are ever full of sap and green" (Ps. 92:14).

One of the Bible's most beautiful promises is that age need not be a barrier to spiritual growth. You can still bring forth fruit in old age, whatever age you consider to be old. This concept of age is one to consider. Children at four or five years of age consider themselves "old" when they enter kindergarten, or soon after when they enter elementary school. It comes middle school time, and twelve-year-olds often think of themselves as old. The truth of the matter is that we age constantly in the sense of calendar reckoning, and as we move through life we are old many, many times. What age is old to the average person? Any age beyond that person's age, that's what old is. Of course there are exceptions to this theory. Some people think themselves into oldness at a very early age and they don't care who is older or younger than they are. They are content with their oldness. They *accept* old, therefore they look and act and feel old. Charles Fillmore has called old age, *"a false belief deeply imbedded in the race mind."* In other words, he suggested that old age is a state of mind. Suggested it you say? Well, not really. He declared it!

In the 20th century longevity among Americans has increased almost 100 percent. In 1900, the average person lived into his 40's. Today, 80 is a more realistic average. Not only are people living longer, but the quality of life is vastly superior to anything any society has ever known before. Predictions for the next century are even more startling in terms of longevity. In fact, some scientists have gone so far as to suggest that by the year 2100 a human being could conceivably live forever. Unity has been teaching eternal life for 100 years. Finally science is catching up. Live forever in body? This was one of Charles Fillmore's goals. He tried valiantly, because he said someone should make the effort; but he made his transition when he was just shy

of 94 years of age. His love for life and his determination to express life to the fullest surely
added many years of productivity and happiness
in his incarnation. He was probably well aware
of another wonderful Bible passage on age: *"Say
not, 'Why were the former days better than
these?' For it is not from wisdom that you ask
this"* (Eccles. 7:10). The good old days? Of
course, they are right now—at whatever age you
are expressing right now. You are exactly as old
as you think you are.

Eric Butterworth coined the perfect expression
concerning age and the idea of old. "My age is
none of my business," he declared. Likewise,
your age is none of your business. People who
defy the calendar with loving, positive thoughts
about themselves stay young. Oh, they observe
birthdays, but they ignore or reject the "piling
up of years" philosophy. Instead of taking a day
off on their birthdays, they mentally take a year
or two off. A husband who forgot his wife's
birthday diplomatically responded: "How do
you expect me to remember your birthdays when
you never look any older?" A birthday doesn't
make you look older. If you look older it is
because you think you should. If you are 80, you
can be 80 years young. It is far better than being
40 years old.

The surest judgment on age is the amount of

inactivity that takes place in the face of a new and divine idea. If new, divine ideas are ignored, then you can be assured old age is setting in. If enthusiastic, energetic, positive effort is put forth to bring new, divine ideas into reality, then you are eternally young.

No matter what our age, old seems to sneak up on us if we are not mentally alert to its pitfalls. Inside of every person who calls himself or herself old is a young person wondering what happened.

Old age is a lie. It is just that, flat out, a lie. As we come to this understanding, our peace of mind level will be greatly enhanced. Our understanding will be on a spiritual, not a physical level. But, you say, isn't it true that our bodies naturally show age as we grow older? It is a fact. It is true the body does show age, but a mature body does not have to be old. In truth, we do not live in our bodies. They are only vehicles for our souls and for Spirit. Of course they are important. We want to take good care of them and see to it that they do their perfect job for us for many, many years to come. But our bodies are not all of us. We truly live in mind. As long as we live positively in mind, we will be young, whatever the physical condition of our bodies might be.

Parade Magazine, in late 1984, had a beautiful

article about myths on aging. It pointed out that most so-called elderly people do not see themselves as old, eight of ten people over 65 can do anything their younger counterparts can do; most older people are more, not less, diverse in life's activities; most older people are perfectly capable of coping with and solving most of life's problems; most older people are less irritable, less demanding, and less critical than their younger counterparts.

Another study, this one reported by *USA Today* in November 1986, revealed that old age doesn't necessarily bring memory loss. Research shows, the newspaper reported, that normal elderly people have minimal deficiencies in memory recall. In fact, memory loss is less than 10 percent that of young people. Why shouldn't the elderly forget more? After all, they have so much more to remember! As for those who declare they have poor memory, the study revealed that many of these people are simply depressed by the demands of modern life, and it follows that they selectively forget what they want to forget. And with a person of any age the least significant and interesting an incident, the more apt one is to forget it. Many who think of themselves as potential Alzheimer victims are really only depressed, the study adds. The year-old study was conducted by J. Michael Williams, a psychiatrist, of Memphis State University.

The loss of peace of mind in connection with advancing years comes down to this: such loss is absolutely unnecessary in a vast majority of situations. People at ages in the 80's, 90's, and even the 100's are perfectly capable of leading active, productive lives. The examples are countless. They include Grandma Moses, Bertrand Russell, George Bernard Shaw, Pablo Picasso, Mary Baker Eddy, the Fillmores, Albert Schweitzer, Michelangelo, Benjamin Franklin, and you, if you choose to make yourself ageless.

For those who say the clock cannot be turned back, the answer is simple: it can be rewound. You can rewind your age clock. You can set it at any age you want to be. Oh, if you are 80, there may be some things that you will not want to try to do that you attempted at age 20, but there will be other things that you will want to try that you didn't attempt at age 20. As we grow older we need to consider less the things we cannot do now that we once did, and be grateful that we are mature enough not to try to do them. We can also be grateful that we are mature enough to know why we shouldn't do some things we used to do.

Charles Fillmore once said: "*Our youth never dies. We let it go to sleep.*" Youth is characteristic of ideas, actions, mental sharpness, success.

To many persons age is characteristic of opposites of these attributes. Tell this to the achievers at advanced ages and they will tell you it doesn't have to be this way. The fact is that older people too often simply let it happen. They believe in the biblical threescore and ten idea. They believe business and industry when it says retirement is mandatory at 65 or 70 "because of old age." They believe the negative conditioning concerning age. The best example, or perhaps the worst example would be a better description, of negative conditioning concerning our age is the lie that as soon as we are born we start to die. Of all false teachings concerning age, this is one of the most damning. Too many believe it and suffer as a result.

When we are born, we start to live a new life. We come into this life from eternal life, and after we end this life by the physical process called death, we enter another phase of eternal life.

The life we are living now is a pause, a comma.

Even so, in the whole scheme of things, it behooves us to live the life we have to the best of our ability. In doing so, we will rejoice with the Psalmist who wrote: *"He asked life of thee; thou gavest it to him, length of days for ever and ever. His glory is great through thy help; splendor and majesty thou dost bestow upon him. Yea, thou dost make him most blessed for ever; thou dost make him glad with the joy of thy presence''* (Ps. 21:4-6).

Whatever age you may be, be at peace! You are exactly the age you need to be at this very moment for your highest spiritual good.

Promises to Keep

Life and Death

"The people who sat in darkness have seen a great light, and for those who sat in the region and shadow of death light has dawned" (Mt. 4:16).

*P*robably no subject warrants more mental attention in the lives of men and women than the subject of death. It is the one great mystery, oddly enough, of life. The Bible abounds with promises concerning death. But more ominous to many people are the threats to men and women concerning the afterlife. An understanding of death seems essential to one's peace of mind, yet how can one understand that which he cannot comprehend and which no one has experienced and returned to tell complete details. Only Jesus tasted death and experienced resurrection, if Christian authorities are correct. Some other religious groups through the recorded periods of civilization have claimed resurrection for certain individuals. Christianity says Jesus Christ is the only one who has attained resurrection. But this is theology. Who is to say who is right and who is wrong? Only God knows of such things. What is important to you, and to me, does not have to do with resurrection at all. What we are concerned about is what is next after this life. The details are not all that important. What we want to know, indeed what we yearn to know, is whether this is all there is! Most of us in what are known as Truth movements, such as Unity, seem to lean toward the possibility of reincarnation. This concept has been called the "doctrine of the second chance" or a "divine possibility" or the most logical explanation of why some live short lives and others long lives and why some suffer throughout a lifetime and others have every need met and often in an extravagant fashion. In this discussion of death, we will not get into a long and involved dissertation on reincarnation. Suffice it to say that it is not considered a fast and hard Unity teaching, but it is safe to say that a high percentage of Unity students believe in it.

What is more important to most people who

are walking the Truth path is the peace of mind that comes when reincarnation, hell, and heaven are simply put out of mind.

One solid Unity Truth and one good affirmation equal peace of mind when death is under discussion.

The Truth is: God is absolute good.

The affirmation: *Whatever happens to us after this life ends just doesn't matter now!*

If God is absolute good, and we teach it and most people who walk the Unity path believe it, *death just doesn't matter!* Whatever takes place after this life will be absolutely good if we have an absolutely good God. And we do have an absolutely good God. God has revealed much of Himself to us through the teachings of Jesus Christ.

One of the most beautiful things He told us is this: *"Truly, truly, I say to you, if any one keeps my word, he will never see death"* (Jn. 8:51).

Does this mean we will not die physically? Of course not. It means we will never die spiritually. This is a promise to keep. Jesus' word is His teachings. Let's be honest, folks. Can anyone keep all the teachings of Jesus Christ? The answer is no. But we can work at keeping them. We can keep more of them today than we kept yesterday. We can be more aware of our need to love, to not make false judgments, to share, to give, to care, and to do that which the Master taught in every respect.

The thing that we must understand is that we are human beings on our way to full spiritual unfoldment. We are not perfect. We make mistakes. Everyone does. To be blunt, if perfection is required for entry into heaven, and if heaven does exist, it will be empty! Who among us will profess to perfection? If one sin, mistake, or error, will get one a sentence in hell, then hell will be so crowded that not even the devil himself will be able to control the traffic. Everyone will be there. Everyone who ever lived, with *no* exceptions. Of course, such a hell cannot exist.

So let's admit it. The concept of heaven and hell is outdated and useless. The fear and reward factors attached to both heaven and hell are of no value to a thinking person.

Another beautiful Bible promise comes to us in the book of Romans, written by Paul:

"For I am sure that neither death, nor life, nor angels, nor principalities, nor things present, nor things to come, nor powers, nor height, nor depth, nor anything else in all creation, will be able to separate us from the love of God in Christ Jesus our Lord" (Rom. 8:38, 39).

Talk about promises! There simply isn't anything anyone can think of that would separate God from His children. Nothing. This seems a good time to be reminded of a promise from the Old Testament: *"Even though I walk through the valley of the shadow of death, I fear no evil; for thou art with me; thy rod and thy staff, they comfort me"* (Ps. 23:4).

Death is a fact of life, but it is not Truth. Physical death is something that takes place in our present consciousness. No one, no matter how holy, is exempt. But it will not always be this way. Perfection is in my future and it is in your future. We are moving in that direction. We are moving toward conscious oneness with the Father and there can be no argument on this point. It is as certain as anything can be certain. This leads us to another wonderful Bible promise from Jesus Christ.

"You, therefore, must be perfect, as your heavenly Father is perfect" (Mt. 5:48).

No promise can be more emphatic. We must be perfect! It is not that we can be perfect. It is not that we might be perfect. We must be. There is no quibbling on the part of Jesus in this respect. He says God is perfect. There is no doubt of that. And we must be perfect as He is!

Again, let's be blunt, and very, very honest. A lot of people have died over the years since Jesus made this dramatic statement. And they died in imperfection. Somewhere, somehow, these people are going on in life to attain the perfection demanded of them by Jesus Christ. There are no details of why or how or where. There is only the blessed assurance that life is going on for those who have already made the transition, and life will go on for each of us after the physical transition we call death.

Charles Fillmore, in *The Revealing Word*, says: *"Death is not a friend but an enemy and must be overcome. Death does not change man and bring him into the resurrection and eternal life. Death has no place in the Absolute."*

Charles Fillmore, Unity's co-founder, is right, of course. He usually is. But he was talking in this context in the absolute. In terms of practical Christianity, death can be a friend. Death is a blessed release to one who is wracked with pain and suffering over a long period of time. Although it may be true that death does not change a person, as Mr. Fillmore suggests, it can give one a new opportunity to express more life.

No better testimony of this truth is available than Paul's when he wrote: *"We are of good courage, and we would rather be away from the body and at home with the Lord"* (2 Cor. 5:8).

Paul had fought the good fight. He was ready to return to God. He was ready to die, in other words. Was he perfect? No, not even Paul would have admitted to perfection. But he was on his way. He had done the work that he had been given to do, and was willing to let the body go so that he might return to God and take another assignment.

This is true of each of us. When we make our physical transitions, we will receive new assignments. The assignments are necessary for us, because they will help us move ever closer to the goal of perfection that Jesus Christ demanded we achieve.

Our own death is always a concern in establishing peace of mind. If we fear death, peace of mind is virtually impossible. Neither should we anticipate it eagerly. Our full attention needs to be placed on living the best we can, *right now*. Sometimes our peace of mind is threatened by our thoughts of death concerning others. We naturally are interested in the lives of those we know and care for, but it is sheer folly to expend valuable mind energy worrying about anything, and especially about something over which we have no control in the first place. The answer to this kind of worry comes back to one of the simplest affirmations: *I trust God*. Have loving concern for those you love, but simply pray for their highest good and let God take it from there. Your peace of mind is at stake!

A man once had a dream about his deceased wife. In the dream, he saw her in angel garb walking in a procession with thousands of other angels. Each angel had a candle which was brightly lighted. His wife's candle was dark. In the dream, he asked her why her candle was not shining. "Your tears," she said, "keep putting my candle out." When the man awoke he knew instantly that the time had come, indeed it was long past, for him to end his grief, dry his tears, and let his beloved wife go on to her highest good.

Grief is natural in death. Diminishing grief is also natural. If grief does not diminish, something is wrong in the person who holds to it. That something must be discovered and dealt with lovingly and positively, or peace of mind is threatened and can even be lost entirely.

A dear friend of mine, whose husband died some time ago, did not let go of grief until she came to an understanding of Truth. With each loving and positive thought and expression of Truth concerning the grief process, she let go a little more. Finally, the process was over. Her peace of mind was restored. She had freed her dear husband, and her tears, symbolically speaking, would no longer hinder his onward march through eternal life.

Promises to Keep

Heaven and Hell

"If I ascend to heaven, thou art there! If I make my bed in Sheol, thou art there!" (Ps. 139:8).

*O*f all our fears, especially in the Christian part of the world, the fear of going to hell must rank near the top. Oddly enough, many others are fearful about heaven. The orthodox view of heaven seems so dull!

Most Christians in years past have been fear-conditioned about hell and have been told that the destination heaven, in the afterlife, is to be desired beyond all other desires. In recent years an increasing number of ministers and church-going people have come, or are coming, to a higher understanding of these pagan concepts of heaven and hell. Unity has been in the forefront in taking the fear out of hell and teaching the truth that hell is a state of mind. One is in hell when one is filled with negative thoughts and feelings and consistently expresses them in actions. On the other hand, one is in heaven when one is filled with loving, positive thoughts and feelings and expresses them in daily activities.

The simple truth is this: heaven and hell are choices. We can choose to be in either state anytime, anywhere. Our degree of peace of mind is dependent upon our choice. If we choose to be in a hellish state, our peace of mind is shaken. If we choose the heavenly state of mind, we soar to new and higher levels of personal peace.

Let's first consider hell, and after finishing with this horrible concept, we will move on to a higher level of consciousness and discuss heaven.

For your peace of mind's sake, for the sake of your very life, it is necessary that you erase from your consciousness the idea of a place of torment and punishment. Many practical Christians have done so. Some find it easy to discredit the idea of hell, but others, who have been heavily conditioned with fear, find it more difficult. Many Truth students still hold on to the possibility that hell exists and that they might have to go there for some earthly mistakes. This cannot be emphasized more strongly: You cannot call yourself a student of Truth and hold onto even a slight belief in a place of punishment called hell. To do so makes you a student of the false, the unreal, the impossible. For, you see, the primary attitude with all valid Truth students is the total belief in an absolutely good God. To believe that absolute good would create such a place is a contradiction in terms. Such belief, even if held minimally, must be released to the oblivion to which it belongs.

The concept of hell is biblical. That much is certain. People who believe in hell (often their belief is strong because they know someone they want to see go there), use the Bible as proof of the existence of this terrible place. You can hear them saying it, "It's in the Bible and that makes it true!" Wrong. It is in the Bible, that much is true; but from there hell begins to take on different shades of color and different degrees of heat. The problem is twofold: translation and interpretation of ancient Scripture texts.

Three words in ancient manuscripts are the basis for the word *hell*: *Gehenna*, *Hades*, and *Sheol*. Gehenna was what we might call today a landfill or junkyard or trash heap. It was the place just outside cities and villages where unwanted things were dumped. Fire burned there constantly to dispose of animal remains and gar-

bage. Hades was a word which meant grave. It
had no other connotation such as fiery or punish-
ing. When one died, one went to Hades, or the
grave. Sheol was a word that correctly could be
translated today as pit. The pit was believed to be
a place of total darkness in death. Not one of
these three words, Gehenna, Hades, or Sheol,
hinted of punishment or fire.

The concept of a fiery hell of punishment came
into being relatively early in Christianity, but was
cemented with the first major English translation
of the Bible. As the translators prepared the
Bible that would ultimately be known as the King
James Version, published in 1611, they faced a
dilemma with the root ancient words that in
English were translated Gehenna, Hades, and
Sheol (pit). What to do with them? For the most
part the answer was simple: let's just call all of
them hell. And, for the most part, this was done.
Thus every known form of afterlife in ancient
manuscripts other than heaven became hell.
Oddly enough, hell comes from the root anglo-
saxon word *helan*, which any dictionary will tell
you originally meant to conceal, hide, or cover
up.

Christianity added the fire, and most likely
this was from the old image of the cleansing,
purifying fires of Gehenna. It also created the
concept of sinners going there for punishment,

greatly assisted by painters with vivid imaginations and writers, such as Dante, with his horrible visions of what hell might be like. Why has Christianity performed such an awful disservice to its followers? Because it served its purpose to do so in years past. It served the mission of orthodox Christianity to keep people in line, to keep them in bondage to fear of punishment and torture if they did not conform to the demands of church leaders. Today, even in orthodox Christianity, hell is seldom mentioned. The reason: there is no longer a valid purpose to keep people in line with fear. The old worn-out dogma of hell has served its purpose, horrible though the purpose might have been. The new purpose: to help people find the state of mind we call heaven, and thereby enjoy peace of mind. The old hellish way was negative. The new heavenly way is positive. Even many of the well-known evangelists of today, who formerly preached hellfire and damnation, have eased off. It is about time.

An orthodox minister, from a fundamentalist organization, said recently in *Newsweek Magazine*: *"Occasionally you'll find a preacher going overboard about Satan and hell, but that's usually someone fixing to have a nervous breakdown."*

But what about satan? What about the devil?

Charles Fillmore calls the devil: *"A state of consciousness adverse to the divine good."* He added: *"The devils that we encounter are fear, anger, jealousy, and other similar negative traits, and they are in ourselves." (The Revealing Word)*

Satan has many names, but no reality. He is called devil, Adversary, accuser, and old man of sin, but he exists only as we allow him to exist in our own minds.

Somehow, somewhere in time, man came into a misunderstanding of God's power and presence. The misunderstanding led to a belief in an opposing power, a power of evil. The devil, or satan, evolved. The evolution is understandable because many cultures and societies of ancient times had such beliefs. The truth is that there never has been and there never will be a power opposite to God. When we affirm: *There is only one power and one presence*, we can do so with absolute conviction of this Truth. Our doing so eliminates a being known as the devil, and puts things in proper perspective. No outside force can mislead us. Only our own negative emotions and feelings and thinking can do so. These have no power in the face of our use of God power.

William L. Fischer, writing in the Unity book, *Alternatives*, says:

"Tremendous cunning and power are attrib-

uted to satan by some people. It is said that sometimes a battle rages between satan and God over the custody of a person's soul. The devil supposedly wins an occasional battle. This is a rather frightening consideration, because it accords more power to satan than to God. It would make us wonder if we have a right to call God 'almighty.' Perhaps if this were the case, we would more appropriately call God 'partly mighty.'"

This is not the case. God is almighty, and as Marcus Bach has written: *"I had to let the devil go when they made him too big. He was bigger than God in many ways, and I had to get him off my back."*

You, too, must get the devil off your back and hell out of your imagination. Your peace of mind depends on it.

What of heaven? Let's consider this transitory quote from James Dillet Freeman, former director of Silent Unity, and widely published author, to get us from a consideration of hell to a commentary on heaven: *"Personally, I find it impossible to accept the traditional notions about heaven and hell. Heaven and hell are real enough as states of mind—I have known people in both. But to believe in hell as an actual place where living souls are tortured eternally, you have to believe in a crueler God than I believe it possible for Him to be.*

"I once had a vision of hell. I was outraged at the thought that the God of love whom I love could create such a place. But as the demon dragged me down into it, he said, 'You don't have the right idea about this place. It is only here because you need it. If you'll look around, you'll see there is no one here except the people you think ought to be here.'

"As to heaven, I pray that we may one day attain it, but perfect bliss would require utter selflessness and perfect love. It is pretty obvious that if we should get into it now, heaven would not long stay heavenly."

More beautiful words on heaven and hell have rarely been spoken, and upon such thinking is practical Christianity based.

Jesus Christ put heaven in perspective for us in many ways and at many times, but the most perfect statement on it ever uttered might well be this one: *"The kingdom of heaven is at hand"* (Mt. 4:17).

Truly the kingdom is at hand, in our very midst, when we claim it as ours in consciousness. It is not a place to go to; it is a place to be in.

So where do we go when we die? The only real answer is: it just doesn't matter. What does matter is the knowing that God is absolutely good. If we know this, and live as if we know it, we do not have to be concerned about how we are going to continue our eternal life. We need only take care of the now, and the hereafter will take care of itself.

So be peaceful about heaven and hell. Come to a mature understanding of the nature of God. And in doing so, your peace of mind is assured.

Look back at the beginning of this chapter and reread the quote, which is from the Revised Standard Version of the Bible. Wherever you are, God is! If you are in hell (Sheol), God is there with you, encouraging you to rise up in consciousness and be all that you can be. If you are in heaven, in perfect peace and harmony, God is there with you, encouraging you to stay there, in mind and action. You are never alone. There is no separation between you and your Creator, now or ever.

Promises to Keep

Forgiveness

"Then Peter came up and said to him, 'Lord, how often shall my brother sin against me, and I forgive him? As many as seven times?' Jesus said to him, 'I do not say to you seven times, but seventy times seven.' " (Mt. 18:21, 22).

*O*ne reason that we do not have peace of mind comes from our failure to forgive. Oh, we forgive others far easier than we forgive ourselves. We are harder on ourselves than we are on those we love—our spouses, our children, our parents. Somehow we feel that no matter what they have done to us that generated pain or discomfort, there is within us a capacity to forgive. But, for ourselves, we go to either extreme, we forgive ourselves too easily or we fail to forgive ourselves at all.

Forgive ourselves too easily? How can this be? Aren't we supposed to forgive ourselves? Yes, we are, but not so easy there. If we consistently repeat the same mistake, and we forgive ourselves over and over without learning the lesson therein, it is not good for our souls. Forgiving and excusing are two different things. When we continually err, and continually forgive ourselves the error, we are making excuses for ourselves. In true forgiveness, a lesson is always learned. A lesson learned should not have to be repeated constantly.

One of the largest barriers to our peace of mind is failure to forgive. The grudges we hold against others and ourselves torment us endlessly. It need not be this way.

Charles Fillmore, writing in a pamphlet that Unity produces called *The Sure Remedy*, gives us a perfect formula for peace of mind in connection with the divine faculty of forgiveness. He called it a mental treatment that is guaranteed to cure every ill that flesh is heir to: *"Sit for half an hour every night and mentally forgive everyone against whom you have any ill will or antipathy. If you fear or if you are prejudiced against even an animal, mentally ask forgiveness of it and send it thoughts of love. If you have accused anyone of injustice, if you have discussed anyone unkindly, if you have criticized or gossiped about anyone, withdraw your words by asking in the silence for forgiveness.''*

What a formula! What a life-saving formula! Oh, if only we would follow it. What peace of mind we would enjoy. A lot of people *do* follow this formula and it leads them to peace. There is no more refreshing way to go to sleep at night than in a state of forgiveness. The awakening hours next morning are ripe with expectation of good. The mind and body are receptive to good. They are clean and free and fresh, ready for good to take place.

Jesus taught us that we are judged as we judge. It follows that we are forgiven as we forgive. What a joy it is to be forgiven an error. But, it is an even greater joy to be able to forgive someone else who has erred against us.

Many people beg God to forgive them. Their pleas are long and loud. Regrettably, this is all a waste.

God is not in the forgiveness business per se. He does not pick and choose who to forgive and who to hold a grudge against. A god capable of such selective discrimination would not be a god worth caring about. A father who forgives one child and refuses to forgive another child is not a fair father. Our God, our Father, would never refuse forgiveness to one of His children. If we could come to this understanding, our peace of mind would soar. We would no longer need to feel guilty, soiled, dirty. We could approach life clean and fresh. Jesus told us to ask forgiveness and it would be ours. Many Truth students have come to the understanding that we don't even have to ask for forgiveness; we only need to claim it. We need to claim our forgiveness. It is ours the moment we claim it. God never withholds His good from His children.

There is the wonderful story, perhaps it is true, about a young soldier who went into battle. When shells started falling, and men dying, the young soldier bolted and ran. He became a deserter. He hid his indiscretion, and years later became quite a famous astronomer. In fact, it is said, he discovered one of our planets. Because of his fame, newspaper reporters started examining his past. It was discovered he was a deserter. Meanwhile, the king of the land where he lived, Great Britain, had announced his intentions of knighting the astronomer. The astronomer dreaded the day when he had to appear before the king, for he knew that even at this late date he could be shot for desertion. But he had to face the king. While he stood outside the king's chambers, awaiting a summons to enter, he stood in dread. But then an assistant came to the astronomer with an envelope and asked him to open it. Inside there was a pardon. There was also a note from the king: "Now we can talk." Thus did the astronomer become a knight, and was forgiven his sin of desertion.

The Truth is this: God is forgiveness itself. God does not forgive; He is forgiveness. It is simply up to us in every situation to accept His forgiveness.

Forgiveness of self and of others is a freeing act.

Unforgiveness is self-imprisonment.

Picture this: Every night in this world thousands, perhaps many thousands, of people go to bed hating and resenting someone or something. They lie in bed tossing and turning, full of vindictive thoughts. The object, or objects, of their scorn are barely aware, and often totally unaware, of their detractor. They sleep peacefully and are not affected by the unforgiveness of another. Whose peace of mind is lost?

Unforgiveness is a lot like acid. A drop of acid makes a small impression on a solid object. Two drops make a greater impression. A flow of acid eats away the surface and digs deeply into the solid object. So it is with unforgiveness. What solid object is most affected by your unforgiveness? You are the most affected solid object. You are scarred, defaced, and even ultimately destroyed by the acid of unforgiveness. Your peace of mind is the major casualty.

Robert Schuller, of Crystal Cathedral fame, has said that resentments are like snowdrifts and forgiveness is like a snowplow. This is so true. Forgiveness opens up our road toward spiritual growth. It removes the barriers that confront us. It permits communication to be restored. It literally helps make the rough places smooth.

Jesus Christ taught us a wonderful forgiveness lesson with the woman who had been adulterous. The Pharisees were trying to trick Jesus, to make Him go against His own teachings of turning the other cheek, of forgiving seventy times seven. They knew the law of Moses. They knew that adultery was a charge which, if proved, would result in automatic death for the woman. Interestingly enough, the man in those Mosaic days usually got off a lot easier than the woman. But Jesus taught the Pharisees a new Truth. In today's terminology, they must have been zapped by this Truth, for they sneaked away. Jesus, of course, told them: *"Let him who is without sin among you be the first to throw a stone at her"* (Jn. 8:7). No one threw a stone. No one. Not even Jesus threw a stone. He might have thrown a stone, if He had wanted to prove to the others that He was an exception, that He was sinless. But He did not. Why did He not even throw a symbolic stone? Because He knew He, too, in His human consciousness, was capable of sin, or making a mistake. Oh, it is doubtful that He was capable of making such a major mistake as the woman had committed, but a mistake is a mistake, and He knew then, as we must know now, that from time to time we all make mistakes. Some seem to make more than others. But we all make them.

The advice to the woman, when He told her to go, after no one felt sinfree enough to stone her, was simple: *"Neither do I condemn you; go, and do not sin again"* (Jn. 8:11). *Neither do I condemn you* must have been words that gave this woman the peace of mind that she had lost in her sin and in her apprehension by the elders. Imagine her fear! Imagine her anxiety! Imagine her torment! Then imagine the Master giving her blessed relief, and see her walking away, determined not to get herself in this kind of mess again. See her becoming all that Jesus Christ could see her becoming. Then, finally, you will begin to understand the wonder and awe of forgiveness and the meanness and the littleness of unforgiveness.

Now picture yourself at this very point in your reading. Recall the mistakes, for that is what sin is really, a mistake, and bring them forth into the light of the Christ. Show them to your own

Christ which indwells you. Let all the ugliness out, for just a moment, and let the Christ examine it.

Then get still. If you listen very carefully, a voice inside you will speak to you, and the words that you will hear are these: "Neither do I condemn you; go, and do not sin again."

Then fall back in blessed relief, just as the woman taken in adultery did, and know you are forgiven. All is well.

Does this mean you will never sin again, never err again? Probably not. As long as we are in the human consciousness, we will make mistakes at times. But every time we do, and we recognize the mistake and accept forgiveness for it, we move ahead. We grow. We expand in consciousness. It is so. It cannot be otherwise.

There is a beautiful cathedral in England with stained-glass windows. Every window is spectacular in beauty. People stand and gaze in great admiration. What is generally not known is that every window is fashioned from bits of broken glass that were discarded. The designer of these windows took something that was ugly, broken, and discarded, and created beauty.

So it is with our lives. We can take the broken, ugly, undesirable things in our lives and turn them into beauty and peace of mind, if we forgive ourselves and learn from our mistakes.

Paul put it in proper perspective: *"But one thing I do, forgetting what lies behind, and straining forward to what lies ahead, I press on toward the goal for the prize of the upward call of God in Christ Jesus"* (Phil. 3:13,14).

What lies behind? Unforgiveness of any kind.

What lies ahead? Total forgiveness, of self, of others.

What is the reward? Peace of mind.

Promises to Keep

Love and Hate

"Hatred stirs up strife, but love covers all offenses" (Prov. 10:12).

*T*his beautiful promise from the Bible can be summed up even more succinctly: hate hurts, love liberates. Hatefulness, spitefulness, meanness of any kind, eat away at our peace of mind. As we convert such negative thoughts and actions to love, our peace of mind is assured.

Before Jesus Christ came into the world, the Ten Commandments and countless other Mosaic laws and regulations prevailed in the hearts and minds of the people. Jesus brought a higher commandment, one which, if followed, would make all other commandments unnecessary. He said:

"This is my commandment, that you love one another as I have loved you" (Jn. 15:12).

The degree of peace of mind in each individual's life is in direct proportion to the obedience level of this commandment.

Legend has it that once a number of men and women decided to go treasure hunting. They had an old treasure map that seemed to be authentic. The site of the treasure, however, was far away in the Pacific Ocean. Nevertheless, they hired a ship and a captain and crew to take them to the treasure island. After many days of travel, the captain shouted to them: "Treasure island!" He continued to shout, but he could not get the attention of the treasure hunters. They were too busy poring over their maps and charts. So, they passed up the treasure island. Days later, the captain again shouted that the treasure island was in sight. Again, he could not get their attention. They were too busy talking about how much treasure they might find. They ignored the captain. Again the island was passed. Still a third time the captain shouted that treasure island was in sight. This time they ignored him because they were too busy talking about how they would share the treasure when they found it. But the story has a happy ending. Finally the captain shouted until they heard him, and the treasure was found and shared, and all lived the proverbially happy ever after.

So it is with love, one of the greatest treasures of all. We pass it up because we are so busy planning to achieve it, because we are so busy measuring the depth of the love we want to achieve, and we are so busy thinking about sharing our love with others so that we might receive in like kind. All the time we are busy, we are passing up the treasure known as love. It might be said we are looking, as the song goes, in all the wrong places.

Love has a starting place. Everything does. Love's starting place is with self. Oh, there are teachers and writers who say that love starts with love of God. Love of God is not an erroneous place to start. It is okay. But it is not the highest and best place to start. For, and it may sound selfish to say this, it is an impossibility to fully love anything or anyone until self-love is accomplished. Until we learn to love ourselves we are incomplete at every level of life, emotionally, physically, spiritually. Without self-love, the most important ingredient in our makeup is missing. When we truly do love ourselves, then we can completely love God and all life.

Somehow through the many hundreds of years since Jesus Christ was with us in body we have been conditioned to put the self down. The traditional church has often described human beings

as worthless worms of the earth. We are pictured
as undeserving even of the love of God. If God is
to love us, the teachings go, we must humble and
belittle ourselves and exalt Him. We must come
to Him on bended knee and plead for His mercy.
What a false teaching this is! It is a teaching
designed to keep people at the mercy of dictato-
rial church leaders.

What is our true nature? *"Yet thou hast made
him a little less than God, and dost crown him
with glory and honor. Thou hast given him do-
minion over the works of thy hands; thou hast
put all things under his feet"* (Ps. 8:5, 6).

Jesus replied, *"Is it not written in your law, 'I
said, you are gods'?"* (Jn. 10:34).

Our true nature is godlike. How ungodlike it is
when we do not love ourselves!

Many years ago it was common misinforma-
tion that the human body, if its chemicals and
minerals could be distilled, would be worth 98
cents. Perhaps this is part of the reason that so
many people think of themselves as worthless. It
might help to know that this information was
never correct. Science now tells us that if all the
latent energy in one human being's cells could be
harnessed and used to generate electricity, one
person could supply all the power the United
States could use for a whole week. The cost of
such energy: an estimated $80 billion dollars.

That makes you worth "godzillions" in potential! Our worth in this respect alone is countless in terms of dollars. A new word had to be coined to register the worth!

Yet so many put themselves down. They refuse to love self, therefore they are incapable of loving God and others. Their inability to love blocks all opportunities for others to love them.

As we learn to love ourselves, we must be very careful. Love of self needs to be at a high level of understanding. We do not want to be arrogant in our self-love. This is not true self-love. It is conceit, untamed ego. True self-love is a great deal more like respect than passion. Self-love, in fact, is passion-less. It is partly physical, for we must love and respect our bodies; but it is primarily spiritual. The love we have for ourselves must be based in terms of spirit, for we are spiritual beings. As we come to this understanding, true self-love is possible and easily attainable. Then the love spreads to everything and everyone in our circle.

"I hate myself," stirs up strife.

"I love myself," covers all offenses.

But what of God's love for us and our love for Him? Unity teaches that of all God's attributes, love is the most beautiful. It is the power that joins and binds us all together in harmony. It is an inner power that sees good everywhere and in everybody. If this is true, why is there so much conflict? Why do so many people dislike, or worse yet, hate each other? The answer is simple, and it is found in the New Testament: *"He who does not love does not know God; for God is love"* (1 Jn. 4:8).

God is love! Does God love us? Of course He does. But here is where all the confusion comes in: God loves us exactly as much as we accept. Some of us are loved more or less, because we accept more or less. God is the principle of love. God is the fountain of love. Your thirst for God's love is quenched as you drink from this fountain. Principle must be used. God wants to be used in every way for our higher good.

Consider the principle of mathematics. This principle is worthless to you unless you use it, right? So it is with God. God's love, God's wisdom, God's strength, God's understanding are yours only to the degree that you accept these qualities.

Those who have learned to love self, love others, and love God know these truths and live them every day in every way possible, to the best of their abilities. When they err, they know exactly what is wrong. They know that somehow through negative thinking or emotions they have blocked the normally clear channel between God and self. When this is discovered, a correction is made, and the flow again comes freely. The flow works in both directions when all is in divine order. In comes love from God's vast storehouse, out go gratitude and praise. Thus the cycle is unbroken, and perfect love is taking place. Peace of mind is the result.

This chapter started with an Old Testament quote on love and hate. Let's end it with a New Testament quote from Jesus Christ: *"You have heard that it was said, 'You shall love your neighbor and hate your enemy.' But I say to you, Love your enemies and pray for those who persecute you, so that you may be sons of your Father who is in heaven"* (Mt. 5:43-45).

Jesus Christ's meaning simply could not be clearer. When we do not love completely we cannot be in heaven. Where is heaven? It is here right now. It is harmony. It is peace of mind. Do we want to dwell in heaven? It follows that we must stop trying to do things the human way, which often includes hatefulness, and do things the spiritual way.

In Jesus' teachings there are many levels of meaning. There are outside examples and there are inside examples. Take, for instance, the teaching in the verse from Matthew just quoted. Do we have enemies? Maybe that is a strong word, but let's use it because the Bible translators gave it to us in this quote. Who is our No. 1

enemy? Without doubt, it is self, when we are not in tune with our true Self. The enemies each of us must love are not so much on the outside as on the inside. We can transform these inner enemies, such as self-doubt, a feeling of worthlessness, and other such emotions, only by love—by loving ourselves enough to want to free ourselves from these enemies. What of the enemies who persecute us? They are negative inner qualities for the most part. What do we do with them? We pray for a transformation of them by the renewal of our minds.

The results are not achieved overnight. As with all good things, all things worth having, patience and diligence are required. But oh, the reward! Peace of mind.

When we achieve this wonderful objective we will truly be living up to the highest commandments Jesus gave us, including: *"You shall love your neighbor as yourself"* (Mt. 19:19).

What a day this will be!

Promises to Keep

Faith and Unbelief

"According to your faith be it done to you" (Mt. 9:29).

*T*his Bible promise is ignored, neglected, or rejected only at the peril of peace of mind. It not only represents a promise, but a law. It is a law akin to reaping as we sow, to being judged as we are judged, and to receiving as we have given.

Someone once described faith as belief without evidence of what is told by one who speaks without knowledge of things without parallel. Doublespeak? Maybe. But, faith, when one expresses it in the truest and the highest sense, can be confusing. Faith requires us to suspend human judgments, human standards, and human conditions. Faith is not of the physical so much as it is of pure Spirit. Most of us dwell primarily in the physical. We are only now coming to a better understanding of who and what we truly are, sons and daughters of the Most High. Oh, we have known it intellectually, but we are coming more to the intuitive, spiritual knowing of this truth. What does it take to come to this understanding? Faith. Or, that which another wag described as "the illogical belief in the occurrence of the improbable." Once when the popular television character Archie Bunker was asked to define faith, he replied: "Believing what you know darned sure ain't so." We may laugh at these innocent attempts to define faith, but that is as far as we should go.

Faith is not illogical, it is not improbable, and it for sure *is so*! It just seems to be otherwise at times. In terms of Spirit, it is totally logical, totally probable. Need we be reminded that with God all things are possible?

Jesus had the right idea about faith. He talked about it a lot. He was an adept student of faith. He lived His faith. He was, as a result, a man with the highest degree of peace of mind that it is possible for one to attain.

What did He tell us?

"Truly, I say to you, if you have faith and never doubt, you will . . . say to this mountain,

'Be taken up and cast into the sea,' and it will be done'' (Mt. 21:21).

Can our faith literally move mountains? Maybe. But it *certainly* can move mountains of negativity. Faith, for people who demonstrate this faculty, moves such mountains every day. The seemingly impossible becomes possible, as faith is put to work.

Faith is almost always preceded by belief. Those who say they cannot find enough faith are really not believing enough. Belief and faith are related, but faith is the higher quality of the two. Belief and faith can free you or imprison you. It is vital for us to demonstrate unbelief at times. It is vital for us to be unfaithful at times. Do not believe that which is false. Do not have faith in that which is false. Doing so assures loss of peace of mind.

If we persistently believe in error, the quality of our lives cannot be as high as we would like it to be. If we believe two plus two equals five, the principles of mathematics will not work for us.

Conversely, if we believe in the ideas of sickness and lack, the principles of life will not work for us.

What we believe in will bring us success or failure. What we have faith in will allow us to retain that which we believe in. It follows that belief in the good, the whole, is what we want, so that we may build a strong faith to retain the good in our lives.

We have opportunities every day, almost hourly, to demonstrate belief and faith, to say yes to the true and no to the false. We can demonstrate faith and belief at every level of being. Perhaps in one moment we are believing in life as a veterinarian tells us a beloved pet may die. Is the veterinarian wrong? No. He may well be right. But do we believe in death? No, we believe in life with all our hearts and minds. We see life where science tells us death may take place. And the pet lives. Our belief has helped it live. Our faith will help *us* to continue to live.

This is not to say that belief and faith always achieve such positive results. Sometimes, no matter how much we believe or how much faith we have, something else is taking place that we cannot know. In such cases, we are still victorious. We have done our part; we have held to the true, the real.

We yield to a wisdom that surpasses all human understanding, and we affirm and accept divine order.

It all comes down to this: *Have faith in God*. God knows what is for our highest good, and as we come to Him in belief, in faith, our highest needs are met.

The results of belief and faith may not always

appear as we would wish on a physical level, but at a spiritual level the results are perfect.

In the wonderful story of *Alice in Wonderland* there is a comment that everyone ought to do three impossible things every morning before breakfast. This doesn't seem logical, but what fun it would be. So it is with faith. It doesn't seem logical, but the results of faith bring us great joy.

What are you facing? Faith it. Faith what you are facing. Faith sickness. Faith lack. Faith misunderstanding. Faith what seems to be to you the impossible.

After you have faithed it, faith it some more.

Sometimes it seems that we have gone down a detour in life so far that we cannot turn around and get back on a path that might lead us to peace of mind. "My life is a mess!" is the plaintive cry. The answer to this life dilemma is to come to a conclusion, once and for all, that you are the "messor"! No one has placed you in a negative situation. You have said yes to that which has put you in the mess you may be in. You have believed in and have had faith in the wrong things and perhaps the wrong people.

A turnaround doesn't just take place. It must be accomplished. You must want to turn your life around and begin to see the life you want. New beginnings don't just happen. They are faithed into being. When you begin to put belief in yourself into effect and faith in God to help you turn your life around, amazing transformations take place.

A little boy was put to bed early one night because of his bad temper. Next morning he arose bright and happy. His mother was amazed at the transformation. "What happened to you?" she asked. He replied: "Yesterday I let my thoughts push me around. Today I am pushing them around."

If you have let your beliefs push you around, begin a new day. You don't have to be aggressive and push the old beliefs around. Gently erase them. Say no to them. Believe in the good and the true, and as your belief system is changed, you will move logically and naturally into new levels of faith.

Silent Unity is built on the premise of faith. Over the years people have come to have faith in the prayers of people in Silent Unity's prayer ministry. This is good. But remember this, for Unity's co-founder, Myrtle Fillmore, said it: *"We appreciate your faith in us, but we want you to have faith in yourself—for God is in you and working through you, just as much as He is in us—and just as much as He is in Jesus Christ." (Myrtle Fillmore: Mother of Unity)*

The faith of Silent Unity works with your

faith. Silent Unity's faith alone cannot do it for you. Your belief, your faith, your prayers, are vital to your peace of mind.

A tramp was once asked his philosophy of life. He replied: "I turn my back to the wind and I go where it blows me." When we go where our beliefs take us, we often find ourselves at an undesirable destination. We need to face the wind, to faith every situation, and in doing so we achieve peace of mind.

Promises to Keep

Success and Failure

"Only be strong and very courageous, being careful to do according to all the law . . . turn not from it to the right hand or to the left, that you may have good success wherever you go" (Josh. 1:7).

The secret of success, according to a formula once put forward by Albert Einstein, is:

$X + Y + Z = A$

A, he said, is success.

X is hard work.

Y is relaxation.

Z, he added with a smile, is keeping your mouth shut.

All too often we talk ourselves out of success.

We think ourselves out of success. We take inappropriate action or we take no action at all. The results, therefore, too often seem to be failure.

In the absolute, failure is not a part of a Truth student's vocabulary. There are, in Truth, only varying degrees of success.

Success, generally speaking, is a favorable or satisfactory outcome. Failure, generally speaking, is falling short, or as Webster defines it: *the state of being lacking, or deficient.* No two people would define these two words in exactly the same manner. There probably are as many degrees of failure and success as there are people.

To a quadraplegic, one step would represent success.

To one without speech, one word would represent success.

To one without hearing, one melody heard would be success.

And for failure? Some children consider themselves failures because they score only 99 on a test. Some adults consider themselves failures because a neighbor has a more expensive car. A man seeking the top government position in this country, the presidency, may be called a failure because he loses by a 51-49 percent vote ratio. Yet, at the same time, this man has been crowned with glory to represent one of the two major political parties and is respected and loved by millions. Failure and success—two very strange animals. The two ways of thinking, that of failure, or that of success, are at the root of much peace of mind or very little peace of mind.

The promise in the Bible, in the book of Joshua, is very plain. We will be successful when we follow the laws of God. Our degree of success will be in direct proportion to the degree in which we follow the laws. If we turn neither to the right nor to the left, our success is assured. Jesus, many years after Joshua's time, took this advice. He set His path on the straight and narrow, keeping God's laws in all His ways. As a result, He healed the blind and the lame and the deaf, and He raised the dead. He went even further: He raised Himself from the dead. Christians ever since have looked to Him as the perfect example of success. A majority of Christians have made Him a figure to be worshiped. A growing minority of Christians, call them practical Christians, if you will, are seeing Him as a figure to be followed, to be emulated. If He did it, they reason, then we can do it, too. They believe His promise: *"Truly, truly, I say to you, he who believes in me will also do the works that I do; and greater works than these will he do, because I go to the Father"* (Jn. 14:12).

If this promise is believed, then why are more

"miracles" not taking place? Why are the blind not being healed? The lame being made to walk? The dead to breathe again?

The New Testament records Jesus as having performed 34 miracles. Today, in the hospital near where you live, ten times as many miracles are taking place. Science and faith have joined hands in a mighty display of what the world generally knows as miracles. The blind are being healed as cataracts are lasered into nothingness. The deaf are being healed as intricate inner ear operations are becoming quite common. The dead are being restored to life and are made to breathe again because of advanced technology that would not have existed if people had not listened to and acted upon divine ideas from an absolutely good God. Jesus did it one way. His way is still effective. People all over the globe are developing, or perfecting, healing powers based in a mighty faith and in obedience to God's laws. Silent Unity and other such prayer ministries in the world witness miracle healings every day. Sometimes the miracle takes place in strictly a faith demonstration. At other times, science works with faith. Is the latter any less a miracle? Of course not. A miracle is a miracle, and a miracle really isn't a miracle anyway. This word *miracle* is confusing. We have come to understand a miracle as something wonderful happening in the face of disaster. We see the something wonderful as abnormal. We see the disaster, too often, as normal. Something is wrong here. Health is normal. Sickness is abnormal. Sickness is really the miracle. It is a miracle that we do not demonstrate the perfection that we are in our real self. But, it will take us many years before most people will come to this understanding; therefore, the word *miracle*, unfortunately, will likely continue to mean to most people an exception to the rule.

A surgeon who once addressed a service club's members said: "There are no atheists in the operating room." He said he had never opened a body for surgery before saying, in some manner, these words, "I know how to do this operation, God. But I want your help." He said he did not know of a single doctor in his wide range of acquaintances who did not similarly practice prayer in such a fashion. "One cannot examine a human body without acknowledging the activity of a higher intelligence at work," he concluded.

Success and failure? The human race is on its way out of failure to recognize the Creator, the Father, and on its way to success in a total realization of the divine relationship between man and God. There can be no turning back.

Jesus told us the way to success is to go to the Father. We are doing it. Some are doing it part-time, some half-time, some are approaching full-time. We will get there. We will not fail. Patience and perseverance are the keys. Nothing is impossible when men and women work with God.

A person was overheard one day musing on "someday my ship is going to come in," and a Truth student asked, "Have you built a pier for it to dock on?" The daydreamer thought for awhile and then, brilliantly, said, "No, but I could swim out to meet it." Oh, what metaphysics are at work here. If our ship is to come in, we must prepare a place for it, and where do we prepare that place first? In mind! We cleanse the mind of ideas of failure and lack and sickness and misunderstanding and create a vacuum for the divine ideas that God is constantly sending to His children. As we cleanse our minds of ideas of failure, we can catch ideas of success. Then, the next action must take place: appropriate activity. Positive, creative, loving activity is mandatory to our success in the face of divine ideas. When we waffle, waver, hang back, success is the most elusive commodity; when we go forward, willingly, eagerly, to meet our good, success is assured.

One of the most blasphemous concepts ever developed is the idea that God's will for us can be failure. If we can imagine God's will for us as failure, we can see ourselves as failures. Would this be God's fault, God's will? Of course not. It would be our mistake. We would have put ourselves into a position to claim failure. God's will for us is to put ourselves into position for success.

Another formula for success is this: When you get a divine idea, act on it. What's more, keep acting until you no longer have to act. Act until you have achieved the success within that divine idea. To do otherwise is akin to trying to climb a ladder with your hands in your pockets. Action, creative, loving, positive action, is the key to success in any walk of life.

Is success spiritual? You bet it is.

"He who conquers, I will make him a pillar in the temple of my God" (Rev. 3:12).

In order to become "a pillar in the temple" we are reminded to keep to the straight and narrow, to keep God first in our lives, to follow the teachings of the good Master, to turn neither left nor right from God's way, to do no harm to other human beings in our pursuit of success, and to deny even the possibility of failure.

No child of God (and we are all children of God) should ever admit to failure. There simply isn't room in God's good world for failure or failures. If we are not demonstrating where we want to demonstrate, then we are on the wrong path. Being on the wrong path is not failure; it is a mistake. Mistakes are made only to be erased, not perpetuated. We are successes if we realize this, if we change (the old word was *repent*) our ways.

Emerson once said: *"The average run of men fret and worry themselves into nameless graves while here and there a great, unselfish soul forgets himself into immortality."*

Immortality, most would agree, is the pinnacle of success. Jesus heads our list of immortals. There are many others on such lists. And what is the number one ingredient in the makeup of an immortal person's being? Service. Oh, Emerson can be misunderstood. Some might say he meant that we should put self down for others. That isn't what he meant at all, and no immortal is worthy of that title who put the self down. Self is important. But what is more important is using ourselves correctly. If we use our talents and abilities to be of service, then we are keeping the kingdom first in our lives, and all things will be ours, including success.

Know this, and your peace of mind is assured.

Promises to Keep

Personal Relationships

"Judge not, that you be not judged. For with the judgment you pronounce you will be judged, and the measure you give will be the measure you get" (Mt. 7:1, 2).

Despite this Bible promise, millions of people attempt to go through life violating it in one way or another. They judge harshly and expect benevolence. They give little and expect a lot. Those who violate this promise do so at the risk of their own peace of mind, and the peace of mind of others. There simply is no way this promise can be ignored and peace be maintained in personal relationships. Those who make every effort to live the instructions Jesus gave truly find the peace that passes all misunderstanding and understanding.

Entire books have been written on personal relationships—thousands of them, in all likelihood. But nothing can improve on the Golden Rule of doing to others as we would have them do unto us.

Too many commit the Golden Rule to memory and forget to commit it to life. In terms of friendships, the Golden Rule is to listen to others as you would have them listen to you. Accept others as you would have them accept you. Approve of others as you would have them approve of you. Free others as you would have them free you.

These tenets seem simple. Perhaps they seem too simple to some people who believe that complexity brings solutions. Complexity brings confusion all too often. Simplicity is always to be preferred in human relationships.

Who will not admit to breakdowns in human relationships? We have all had far too many such situations in our lives. We do not want a continuation of such challenges. What is the solution? It is one word: *commitment*. Each of us must make a commitment to what is right and true and stay with it in the face of all appearances to the contrary.

Someone once made up a list of the ten most

beautiful words in the English language. The word friend was not on that list. The list was obviously incomplete. No list of most anything that is good can exclude friend.

On the other hand, someone once made up a list of the ten harshest words in the English language. When Carl Sandburg saw the list, he said one word is missing. He called it the worst word in the world: *exclusion*.

He was right. Exclusion builds walls, shuts people out, makes them know they are unwelcome, even undesirable. The word *friend* and the word *exclusion* are totally incompatible. Friends are warm and inviting; exclusion is harsh and demeaning.

Who is your friend? Every person on this globe is your friend in potential. Every person on this globe is your brother or sister in Truth. No one deserves exclusion; everyone deserves friends.

Eric Butterworth has said that happy relationships depend not so much on finding the right people, but in being the right person.

Getting along with people, developing good human relationships, depends about two percent on the kind of person they are and ninety-eight percent on the kind of person you are.

A woman was once heard to say, "I am beholding the Christ in (name omitted) but I am

having to strain!" It is true that the Christ indwells every human being. There can be no argument about that. It also seems to be a fact that
the Christ is difficult to see in some people who
consistently violate spiritual and physical and
man-made laws. But the Christ is always there, in
every human being. There are no exceptions. If
we must strain to see it, then to strain is good.
For we must come to this basic understanding.

Does this mean we accept the murderer? The
rapist? The thief? It does. It means we accept
them, but we reject their behavior. We love, so to
speak, the individual and reject his expression if
it is of a negative nature. A person is punished by
the violations of God's law. God's law punishes
no one. A person, it also follows, is punished by
the violations of man's laws. Man's laws punish
no one. The law, man-made or of God, is neu-
tral. It neither punishes nor rewards. Following
law brings reward. Violating law brings punishment.

These are important things to remember in our
personal relationships. We are to judge righteously, or correctly. If we do so, our relationships are wonderfully rewarding. If we do not
judge righteously, or correctly, pain and loss of
peace of mind are sure to take place.

Most people would not want to be friends with
a murderer. This seems reasonable. But to hate a

murderer is unreasonable. It is unhealthy. It is pure and simple error.

But, most of us do not have to make such choices. We live in an ordinary, everyday world where, generally speaking, those who come into our sphere of influence are ordinary, everyday people. Some of these people become close to us. Others do not, for one reason or another. We judge this person as friend material. We judge another as acquaintance material. We may judge even another as an object of love. All such judgments are valid when done *righteously*. Righteously is the key in our determination of who will become close to us and who will remain distant. What is more, it is not only valid, but right and proper for us to say no to some relationships. No can often be very positive and for our highest good and the highest good of the other person involved.

As the story goes: He proposed, she said no, "and they both lived happily ever after." The point is this: When we say no in a relationship it must be a righteous no. It must be, if it is a good decision, based on reasons other than false judgment.

Some people take the quote from Jesus about judging too literally. They think all judgments are wrong. This thinking is untrue. We must make judgments every moment of every day simply to survive. We make a judgment when we cross a street that we can safely make it to the other side before the traffic reaches us. Countless other such decisions are made. When we make right decisions, we are safe, secure, and our peace of mind is intact. When we judge falsely, we do not fare so well. So it is in personal relationships.

If we want a peaceful and loving environment in which to live we must come to grips with the divine idea behind good personal relationships. People getting along with people is the answer to virtually every human problem one can name. Wars start because people do not get along with people. Marriages and friendships end because people do not get along with people.

If our world is to continue to survive and thrive, it is necessary for us to be mindful of a truth: We cannot be personal friends with everyone, but we must not be personal enemies with anyone. When we come to understand that everyone is a potential friend we will find peace. It will elude us as long as we perceive anyone as a potential or real enemy.

"Oh, I know that!" is often the answer when Truth is spoken. "Oh," they say, "that is basic. Give me something deep and profound. That stuff doesn't work in my relationships."

A pity. "That stuff" all too often is never

given a fair chance. Why? Because it is so simple. Anything so simple as seeing everyone as a potential friend is believed pollyannish! Not at all. It is Truth, and if each of us would work on this truth with all our energy and with a full commitment to brotherhood, it is an objective within reach.

Brotherhood or sisterhood, what a worthy objective. It is possible. It is close. Oh, so very close.

"Let there be no strife between you and me . . . for we are kinsmen" (Gen. 13:8).

Truly we are linked in this journey through life, each of us. We are neighbors. The law Moses gave us and the law Jesus reminded us of is simple: "Love your neighbor."

Love brings relationships that satisfy, that give us peace of mind. Believe it! Live this mighty truth.

Promises to Keep

A New World

"For behold, I create new heavens and a new earth; and the former things shall not be remembered" (Is. 65:17).

God has promised us a new earth, but it is up to us to bring it forth. In the beginning the earth was created along with all other creation in the name of good. In the absolute the earth is good, and all its inhabitants are good. But humanity, especially, has misused powers and misdirected energies and talents and abilities with a resulting earth that sorely needs a transfusion, a transformation. It is time for the old world to pass away and a new world to be birthed. The process is well underway.

There is in this time and place renewed interest in our tired old world. There is interest in an ever-increasing number of people that the process cannot be put off any longer. The peace of the world is at stake on a collective level and our own peace of mind is at stake at a personal level.

World peace is the need and world peace is going to be achieved. But how?

Some people believe that if enough people at one time and one place pray for peace, visualize it, then the scales will be tipped in the direction of peace and away from conflict. This may be true, but if it is true it will be so because the people at that one time and place are doing more than just praying for peace. They must be *living* for peace.

Jesus said: *"Why do you see the speck in your brother's eye, but do not notice the log that is in your own eye?"* (Mt. 7:3).

Too many appear to have this problem concerning world peace. They see the injustice and inharmony in the world, but they do not recognize it in themselves. No matter how many times we go into prayer for world peace, unless we take peace into the world, we will not achieve our objective.

The year 1986 was officially the International Year of Peace, so designated by the United Nations. In that same year, the Associated Press estimated in a story circulated in November that the nations of the world spent $900 billion dollars on weapons of war. This is about $1.7 million dollars a minute. Further, since 1960, the Associated Press says, the world nations have spent $14 trillion on weapons. The United States ranks first; the Soviet Union second in the awful race to destroy and kill. The U.S. spent $268 billion and the Soviet Union spent $237 million in 1986, if these figures are accurate.

How much did the nations of the world spend on peace? Some would say that an investment in weapons is also an investment in peace. Maybe so. But it shouldn't have to be this way, and it simply will not be this way in the new world which is to come. We will have grown past this infantile idea of needing to carry a bigger club with which to protect ourselves.

When is this world coming? This is uncertain. The certainty is this: it is coming. We, all of us, now have a place in helping to make it come about.

Good parents do not always live long enough to see their children grow up. They do not always live long enough to see grandchildren and great-grandchildren grow to maturity. But this does not keep them from giving their best efforts to assure the success, health, prosperity, peace of mind, and well-being of their heirs. By the same

token those of us on earth at this time may not
see world peace in our lifetimes, or even the
lifetimes of our children or grandchildren, but
we can know with all assurance that our efforts
in that direction will not go unrewarded. Just as
children grow up and mature, so will our world.
When it does, we can be sure that no investment
of $900 billion will be necessary for weapons.
More, much more than that amount, will go
toward permanent peace.

*"They shall beat their swords into plowshares,
and their spears into pruning hooks; nation shall
not lift up sword against nation, neither shall
they learn war any more"* (Is. 2:4).

To paraphrase: We will turn our attention
toward things of peace and away from things of
war.

Despite all appearances to the contrary, this
very process is now taking place. Little by little,
we are learning the folly of war.

William James, the great philosopher, said in
The Will to Believe: *"The war against war is going to be no holiday excursion or camping party.
The military feelings are too deeply grounded to
abdicate their place among our ideals until better
substitutes are offered . . . ."*

What are better substitutes? Peace feelings.
Every time in every way, peace feelings must replace the feelings of militancy.

James also said, in *Memories and Studies:* *"The deadliest enemies of nations are not their foreign foes; they always dwell within their own borders."*

What a truth this is! In the absolute, in the practical, in the physical, in the spiritual realms, this is always true. The enemy lies within. The enemy is always in reality negative thoughts and emotions and actions.

For almost two thousand years men and women of traditional Christian faith have looked to the return of Jesus Christ to herald the new age, the new earth. Ah, but it is a mistake. He is not returning in body. He does not need to. He never left *in spirit.*

"Lo, I am with you always" (Mt. 28:20).

The Spirit of Jesus Christ, the perfect man, indwells all of us. The Christ within speaks softly, but the Christ speaks surely. The voice says to us, if we would but hear it, *"peace."*

Charles Fillmore said, in his wonderful book that was written far ahead of its time, *Atom-Smashing Power of Mind: "The world needs the Christ consciousness. The need implies that the attainment is near at hand . . . . The Prince of Peace should be invited to the peace conferences that are held by war-taxed and war-weary peoples."*

He further added that when we have the Christ

Spirit pointed out to us, as a race, then the only ambition men and women will have is to compete in bringing forth Truth, goodness, and righteousness.

When all people everywhere compete in the name of goodness, the new age and a new world will be upon us.

Sickness, lack, misunderstanding, and all other such limiting conditions will no longer have a place in our lives.

Does this sound Utopian? It sure does. Do you want to be a part of such a world? It is certain that you do. What is your part in seeing that such a world comes into being?

It is simply this: Look beyond appearances. Even when the world situation looks bleak in terms of peace, we must hold to the good, to the true, to the real. We must go neither right nor left on our journey toward realization of a peaceful world. We must stay on the straight and narrow.

If we hold to the idea of peace, as did Myrtle Fillmore, we yet may see the day she envisioned:

"We are praying for the glad day when the warships shall be turned into schoolhouses and love shall become ruler in the hearts of men." *(Myrtle Fillmore: Mother of Unity)*

That day is upon us. Hold to this truth and do not let it go. World peace need not be a dream; it can and will be a reality with our loving affirmations.

What can you do? You can be a peacemaker in all your ways, and know that this, another wonderful Bible promise, is the reward:

"Blessed are the peacemakers, for they shall be called sons of God" (Mt. 5:9).

Part Three

The Peace That Passes All Understanding

"And the peace of God, which passes all understanding, will keep your hearts and your minds in Christ Jesus" (Phil. 4:7).

The peace of God, which passes all understanding, and also all misunderstanding, is the key to peace of mind.

"I can do it alone," simply won't wash.

We cannot do it alone. Our attempts to do it alone, selfishly, greedily, in conflict, have resulted in torment and suffering. Just as there are no atheists in operating rooms, where the inner splendor and magnificently created organs of life are exposed, it follows that there literally cannot be any atheists in a universe of such munificent good. All that there is, is created in beauty and good. Divine order rules our universe and all the life-forms in it. Perfection in nature is the rule, never the exception. Where there seems to be an exception, it is in perception.

The beautiful passage in Philippians, which began Part III, is followed immediately by one of the most spiritual messages in the Bible:

"Finally, brethren, whatever is true, whatever is honorable, whatever is just, whatever is pure, whatever is lovely, whatever is gracious, if there is any excellence, if there is anything worthy of praise, think about these things" (Phil. 4:8).

No two consecutive verses in all the Bible pack more truth and power than these two. If you want to enjoy the pearl of great price, you must pay the great price. You must first seek the peace of God, which passes all understanding, and in doing so you must seek in true, honorable, just, pure, lovely, gracious, excellent *ways*.

We cannot attain peace of mind by selfish means. The leaders of nations of the world in our recorded past must surely have taught us this. Every selfish endeavor is doomed to failure. So it is that when we seek the peace that passes both understanding and misunderstanding we must do so in absolute unselfishness.

A key passage from the Lord's Prayer (found in chapter six of Matthew) gives us these words of destiny: *"Thy kingdom come, thy will be done, on earth as it is in hevaen."*

From this it is clear that Jesus Christ was telling us that heaven must be brought to earth. The kingdom must be brought to earth. He literally decreed, affirmed, that it take place. He knew of what He spoke. There are no hidden meanings here.

Some persons have gone so far as to suggest that the entire Sermon on the Mount, constituting chapters five, six, and seven of Matthew, is a blueprint for bringing the kingdom on earth into reality. The plan, if followed, would insure that it take place. Look at the sermon.

It tells us of our wonderful blessings when we follow the laws of God.

It tells us we, human beings, are the salt of the earth and a light to the world.

It tells us the wonderful values of brotherhood.

It tells us that the straight and narrow path is difficult, but ever so rewarding.

It tells us to love everyone, even our enemies.

It tells us how to give and how to receive.

It tells us how to pray, and to whom.

It tells us to live today, without anxiety about tomorrow or regret about yesterday.

It tells us how to judge, how to ask, what to seek, how to judge a true prophet, how to find the way to eternal life, and oh, ever so much more. The three chapters, if properly understood and *lived*, can change every hellish situation into pure harmony.

Truly, the peace that passes all understanding can be found and obtained by anyone bold enough to take the Sermon on the Mount into his or her heart and mind.

One of the most strident questions asked by street-corner Christians is: "Have you been born again?" The idea of being born again in traditional Christianity involves being "saved," confessing sins, and accepting Jesus Christ as savior and Lord. It stems from a quote in John: *"Truly, truly, I say to you, unless one is born anew, he cannot see the kingdom of God"* (Jn. 3:3). Jesus went on to say that the new birth must be of Spirit. In other words, we must move from physical understanding to spiritual understanding, from physical expression, to spiritual expression. Then we will be able to *see* the kingdom of God. Anything we can see, anything we can visualize, or imagine, we are capable of achieving. We must be able to see the kingdom of heaven before we may enter it.

The earth, also, must be born anew. Whether it does so is entirely dependent upon its citizens being born again into the spiritual life and away from the physical and material life. This does not exclude the physical (or the material). It simply puts everything in proper perspective, with things of Spirit in the forefront.

In the old life of misunderstanding, we selfishly sought out personal pleasure and material gain. In the new life of understanding, we will seek to be of service, to love unconditionally, to keep the kingdom first, with the assurance that all things necessary for the good life will be added.

Our previous misunderstanding, that of putting fame, fortune, power, success, and other such desires first in our lives will no longer be possible. We will know our priorities. The raucous roar which tells us at times to be self-centered, mean, and little will be stifled. The still small voice that brings peace of mind will be our constant guide.

Do you want to live in such a world? How much do you want to live in such a world?

The price is high. To some it is too high. Will you pay the price?

Here it is:

Keep God first in your life in all your ways.

Follow the teachings of Jesus Christ to the best of your understanding and ability.

Love God, love all the people on this planet, and love yourself.

That's it. Oh, so simple.

The destiny of this earth is at stake. Peace in the world is at stake. Peace of mind is at stake—yours and everybody else's.

Will you do your part to turn all misunderstanding into understanding? Will you know this for yourself, and for every other human being: *"Christ in you, the hope of glory"* (Col. 1:27)?

If you will, the new you and the new earth are both on their way to becoming new realities.

Peace!